# A COMPENDIUM OF RESEARCH ON INFORMATION AND ACCOUNTING FOR MANAGERIAL DECISION AND CONTROL IN JAPAN

# A COMPENDIUM OF RESEARCH ON INFORMATION AND ACCOUNTING FOR MANAGERIAL DECISION AND CONTROL IN JAPAN

Edited by
Seiichi Sato, Yokohama National University
Kyosuke Sakate, Soka University
Gerhard G. Mueller, University of Washington
Lee H. Radebaugh, Brigham Young University

Editorial Advisors
Kiyoshi Kurosawa, Yokohama National University and Dokkyo University
Otojiro Kubota (deceased), Kobe University

International Accounting Section

American Accounting Association

Library of Congress Catalog Number: 82-70970
ISBN 0-86539-040-1
Printed in the United States of America

American Accounting Association
5717 Bessie Drive
Sarasota, Florida 33583

CONTENTS

Page

## PREFACE

In December 1977, the International Accounting Section of the American Accounting Association was approached (with encouragement from Professors Sato and Mueller) by Professor Kyosuke Sakate, who was then a Visiting Scholar from Soka University at the University of Washington, about the possibility of publishing a series of articles on management decision and control in Japan. These articles were primarily to be written in Japanese and translated into English so that scholars from around the world would be exposed to management accounting thinking in Japan. Approval for the project was granted in November 1978. At that time, Professor Sakate, with active assistance from Professor Sato, began the task of selecting authors and articles and having the articles that were originally written in Japanese translated into English. The articles were completed and delivered to the Section in 1980. After necessary editorial reviews and adjustments, the articles were ready to be retyped and published in 1982.

Some of the articles were written in English by Japanese scholars specifically for this Compendium. Because of space and cost constraints, three of the articles are published here in abstract form, and special thanks go to Professors Fushimi, Itami, and Tsuji for allowing us to publish the abstracts instead of the completed articles. Anyone interested in complete copies of the articles should write Professors Fushimi, Itami, and Tsuji at their addresses found in the Biography section.

The problem of translating technical material from one language into another is complex. Editing of translated materials is especially difficult when the editor doesn't have access to the original articles and couldn't read them even if he did! Obviously, many difficulties were encountered and had to be resolved.

However, the project is definitely worthy of these efforts. It is the first of its kind for the AAA International Accounting Section and is, in fact, something rarely done in academic accounting circles. Special praise goes to Professor Sakate whose patience and hard work made this effort possible. In addition, special thanks are given to Diann Porter and others for the Herculean task of retyping all of the articles once they were edited and Scott Florence for assistance in proofreading.

Lee H. Radebaugh
Past Chairman
International Accounting Section
American Accounting Association

ACKNOWLEDGEMENTS

This collection consists of eleven papers which represent the current state of the art in the field of management accounting and information systems in Japan. Many of them are quantitative analyses and represent the fruits of recent developments in the management sciences applied to accounting and information systems for management decision making and control. The authors are all competent scholars in Japan who are well recognized in our academic circles. I am heartily pleased with the publication of this work as a collection of their endeavors.

In the past, Japanese scholars in accounting have exerted themselves to achieve international and cultural exchanges with American scholars in several ways. Some have published papers in American professional journals. A number of Japanese students and researchers have studied at American graduate schools. Many professors in Japan have attended the AAA's annual meetings. Recently this attendance from Japan has increased. In 1979, Professors Seigo Nakajima and Yukio Fujita made presentations, as Japan Accounting Association representatives, at an international accounting concurrent session at AAA's Honolulu meetings.

Under these circumstances, the publication of this collection is timely. Not only will it make a significant contribution to the area of Japanese management accounting and information systems, but it will also be of great use in conveying current Japanese academic accounting interests and the state of the art to colleagues in the United States and other English-speaking countries. It is my firm belief that the Japan Accounting Association will continue in the future to make sustained efforts to promote active international exchanges with accounting scholars all over the world.

Shigeo Aoki, President
Japan Accounting Association

It was with great pleasure that I assented when Gerhard Mueller asked me to accept a role in this most significant project.

Through the years we have welcomed many Japanese professors to the meetings of the American Accounting Association and many have studied at various universities in this country. As of 1981 there are 314 AAA members in Japan plus 32 Japanese student associate members. Also, many of us from the United States have had the pleasure of visiting and teaching at some of the universities in Japan. My experience as a visiting professor in Japan was professionally rewarding for me, and most enjoyable for my entire family. However, there have been all too few opportunities for professors from our two countries to cooperate on specific projects. Also there has been very little Japanese research on business subjects translated into English. Thus, this is an important and exciting effort, and we hope there will be many more cooperative ventures in the future.

We in the AAA express our deep appreciation to all the researchers and authors who contributed to this work and to Professors Mueller and Radebaugh and other members of our International Accounting Section who conceived the idea and have brought the concept to reality.

Donald H. Skadden
Past President
American Accounting Association

I am gratefully pleased to have a new addition to our field in the form of a publication entitled "A Compendium of Research on Information and Accounting for Managerial Decision and Control in Japan." The original idea for this publication was fostered by Professor Gerhard G. Mueller at the University of Washington where one of the faculty members of our university, Associate Professor Kyosuke Sakate, conducted research as a Visiting Scholar.

In my capacity as Professor of Accounting, I am convinced that this type of interdisciplinary and internationally oriented research has significant value for further development of the field of management science. Moreover, this project is very timely. As a world community of scholars we have increasing needs for international exchanges of the results of our respective academic efforts.

There is a saying "Scientific disciplines have no boundaries." Thus, scientific interchanges among countries should be facilitated. May this publication project be a significant step in that direction for the field of accounting.

Kazuo Takamatsu, President
Soka University
Professor of Accounting

Twenty years ago, the field of international accounting did not exist. Since then it has solidly established itself as a curriculum component in accounting education at colleges and universities, garnered a substantial portion of the accounting literature, attracted outstanding researchers to its classification and analysis and challenged the imagination of many leaders of the profession.

This compendium represents yet another pioneering advance for the international accounting discipline. It is a giant step toward the age-old dream of a functioning international community of scholars. All along, language barriers have no doubt been the worst obstacles to continuous and comprehensive international scholarly communications.

Publication of the present compendium demonstrates that recognized scholars, working in one particular language and cultural setting, can transfer their work to those similarly engaged in other settings. The potential benefits from interchanges of this type are likely to be substantial. Thus, I personally welcome the publication of these 11 contributions by Japanese colleagues to the English-language pool of accounting literature. It is my hope that similar publications extending to still other language areas will follow in due course.

It is an honor to have been associated with this project from its very inception.

Gerhard G. Mueller
Past Chairman, Advisory Board
International Accounting Section
American Accounting Association

In academe as well as practice, management uses of decision-relevant information are a matter of concern to which we have paid increasing attention. Most Japanese approaches to the subjects of management accounting and information theory owe much to the significant contributions made by researchers in the United States, European countries, and elsewhere.

There are two basic lines of thought underlying investigations concerned with managerial uses of information in Japan:

* First, intensive research has been conducted on an *a priori* theoretical basis as well as empirically utilizing fundamental concepts accepted world-wide.
* Second, theoretical inquiries have been made on the background of actual business practices in our society which incorporate inherent behavioral patterns and national styles of enterprise decision-making.

It seems that a third decision is quite promising as the 1980's begin. In the past, Japan has often "imported" fundamental modes of analyses or inductively developed pragmatically derived propositions. Now, both of these approaches may be extended in a search for indigenous Japanese variables which, if identified and verified, may expand and further refine existing pure and applied theory.

This Compendium is the first of its kind to be introduced *abroad* in the form of collected papers. The collection covers the field of managerial accounting and information theory as far as we know and use it in our professional activities.

The publication of this work has its origin in Professor Gerhard G. Mueller's suggestions made during the summer, 1977 in Seattle. We are indebted to him for his support and guidance. Our sincere thankfulness goes to the American Accounting Association, especially its International Accounting Section, for giving us the valuable opportunity to realize this project. We also wish to express our gratitude to Professor Lee H. Radebaugh, past chairman of the Section, and Professor Shigeo Aoki, President of the Japan Accounting Association, for their continued encouragement and assistance. The editors also are grateful to the authors who have made original contributions to this publication or given permission to reproduce earlier significant papers.

Seiichi Sato, Professor
Yokohama National University
and
Kyosuke Sakate, Associate Professor
Soka University

## BIOGRAPHY OF AUTHORS

FUSHIMI, Tamio
Graduate School of Business Administration
Keio University
1960 Hiyoshi-honcho, Kohaku-ku
Yokohama 223, JAPAN

Tamio Fushimi is Professor of Business Administration at the Graduate School of Business Administration, Keio University. Formerly he taught at the Engineering School of the same university. He received his B.A. (1958), M.A. (1960) and Ph.D. (1972) degrees from Keio University. His main teaching and research areas are Management Control, Managerial and Engineering Economics, and Management Accounting.

HIRADATE, Michiko
Faculty of Economics
Kanazawa University
1-1 Marunouchi
Kanazawa 920, JAPAN

Michiko Hiradate is Professor of Statistics on the Faculty of Economics at Kanazawa University. He graduated from the Graduate School of Economics at Tokyo University in 1966 and also studied Mathematics in Poland from 1959-1960.

ITAMI, Hiroyuki
Faculty of Commerce
Hitotsubashi University
Kunitachi
Tokyo 186, JAPAN

Hiroyuki Itami is currently Associate Professor in the Department of Commerce at Hitotsubashi University. He holds a B.A. from the same school, and M.S. and Ph.D. degrees from Carnegie-Mellon University. His research interests range from management control and analytical methods in management accounting to economics of internal organization and corporate strategy. He has contributed in the past to The Accounting Review, Journal of Accounting Research, Management Science and various Japanese journals, and authored a monograph from The American Accounting Association.

KOBAYASHI, Kengo
Department of Economics
Shiga University
1-1-1 Banba-cho, Hikone-shi
Shiga 522, JAPAN

Kengo Kobayashi is Professor of Management Accounting at the Shiga University. He holds a Ph.D. degree from the City University of Osaka. He is the author of the following books: Direct Costing, Profit Management in Custom Made Product Company, and Cost Accounting.

KOBAYASHI, Tetsuo
School of Business Administration
Kobe University
Rokkodai-cho, Nada
Kobe 657, JAPAN

Tetsuo Kobayashi is Professor of Accounting at the School of Business Administration, Kobe University. He received an MBA (1960) and a Ph.D. (1973) in business administration from Kobe University. He has published three books, including Cost Theory (1972) and Cost Accounting for Performance Evaluation (1974), and numerous research papers.

His current research interests are in the design of management accounting systems based on structure matrix and in the trade off between efficiency and equitability which accounting information induces.

MIYASAWA, Koichi
Faculty of Business Administration
Soka University
1-236 Tangi-cho, Hachioji
Tokyo 192, JAPAN

Since retiring from University of Tokyo in 1965, Koichi Miyasawa has been Professor of Management Science at Soka University. In 1960-1961, he studied Game Theory as a Fulbright Research Scholar at the Econometric Research Program, Princeton University and in 1964-65 he engaged in joint research work on Decision Theory with the late Professor Jacob Marshack at Western Management Science Institute, University of California, Los Angeles. His research results were published in Advances in Game Theory, Management Science, and International Economic Review. He has also been involved in the activity of the International Institute for Applied System Analysis since the establishment of the institute in Vienna in 1972.

MIZOGUCHI, Kazuo
School of Business Administration
Kobe University
Rokkodai-cho, Nada
Kobe 657, JAPAN

Kazuo Mizoguchi is Professor of Accounting at the Kobe University and holds a Ph.D. degree from the same university. He was given the "Ohta" award by the Japan Accounting Association in 1955. He has been a Visiting Professor at the Goettingen, Muenster and Muenchen Universities in West Germany. He is the author of books in managerial accounting, cost theory, and cost accounting.

MONDEN, Yasuhiro
School of Economics
University of Osaka Prefecture
Mozu, Umemachi, Sakai
Osaka 591, JAPAN

Yasuhiro Monden is Associate Professor of cost/management accounting at the University of Osaka Prefecture, and during 1980-81 was a visiting associate professor of accounting at State University of New York in Buffalo. He holds an M.B.A. degree from Kobe University. He is author of the book: *Multi-Goal, Multi-Level Management Accounting* (Dobunkan, Tokyo 1978).

OKAMOTO, Kiyoshi
Faculty of Commerce
Hitotsubashi University
Kunitachi
Tokyo 186, JAPAN

Kiyoshi Okamoto is Professor of Accounting at Hitotsubashi University in Tokyo. He holds a Doctor of Commerce degree from the same university and studied at the University of Michigan as a Fulbright grantee in 1965-1966.

OHNARI, Setsuo
Faculty of Commerce
Hitotsubashi University
Kunitachi
Tokyo 186, JAPAN

Setsuo Ohnari is Professor of Mathematics at Hitotsubashi University, teaching mathematics in management. He holds a Master of Science degree from Tokyo University.

SAKATE, Kyosuke

Faculty of Business Administration
Soka University
1-236 Tangi-cho, Hachioji
Tokyo 192-01, JAPAN

Kyosuke Sakate is Associate Professor of Accounting at Soka University. He holds an M.B.A. degree from Kobe University, and he studied at the University of Washington as a Visiting Scholar in 1977-78. His current interests in research are in establishing application sets of input-output analysis to managerial accounting problems and he is the author of "Cost Accounting" (1978).

SEKIYA, Sho

Graduate School of Business Administration
Keio University
1960 Hiyoshi-honcho, Kohoku-ku
Yokohama 223, JAPAN

Sho Sekiya is Associate Professor of Managerial Economics in the Graduate School of Business Administration at Keio University. He graduated from Tokyo University, Graduate School of Economics in 1964 and participated in the 1968-69 International Teachers' Program of the Harvard Business School.

TSUJI, Masao

School of Commerce
Waseda University
6-1 Nishiwaseda 1-chome, Shinjuku-ku
Tokyo 160, JAPAN

Masao Tsuji is Assistant Professor of Decision and Information Systems at Waseda University in Tokyo. He received his B.A. and M.A. in commerce from Waseda University and C. Phil. in management from UCLA. He is a member of the AAA and TIMS.

# A CONTROL MODEL FOR SIMPLE HIERARCHICAL ORGANIZATIONS

By Sho Sekiya and Michiko Hiradate

## 1. Introduction

Generally speaking, there seems to be an important distinction among decision variables in an organization. One is a group of such variables which have direct effect on various objectives in the organization. The other is a group of decision variables which have only indirect relations to the objectives of the organization through changing the organizational structure and yet have considerable effects on the ultimate objectives.

In the usual decision analysis setting, it is natural for us to consider the structural effects of the organization as being divided into two parts. One is the effect of a so-called "information structure" or a system for recognizing information inside and/or outside of the organization, and the other is the effect of human or motivational factors within the organization which should be ultimately reflected in the preference function of the decision units.

In our discussion, for the sake of simplicity, we will neglect effects of the former system and confine ourselves to effects of changing the latter. As for the former, much attention has been paid thus far, and many fruitful theoretical concepts and results have been well developed. However, there has been much negligence in decision variables of the latter. There seems to be two reasons why such negligence has been prevalent. One reason might be due to the concentration of research efforts on the study of teams, and, from the very definition of teams, these kinds of problems should have been discarded. Another reason might be the implicit assumption usually made in the analysis of financial decisions for the business firm; the assumption of the risk neutrality of top executives who should reflect the numerous stockholders' interests. But, this kind of assumption seems to be self-deceptive when we simply observe the actual behavior of business firms. At least in Japan, although the number of stockholders is large, the actual behavior of business firms is determined by the interests of a handful of stockholders, i.e., financial institutions, and the overall preference function, if it exists, is determined by the de facto stockholders.

## 2. The Model

Suppose there is a simple hierarchical organization which is composed of one corporate or a central unit and its two divisions operating as profit centers under different environmental conditions. These divisions, which will be referred to as Division 1 and Division 2 respectively, are assumed to earn an uncertain return of $x_1$ and $x_2$ on each \$1.00 invested. Furthermore, the central unit should exercise control over the divisions by changing various organizational structures as well as sending ordinary parameters for capital allocation. The net effect of these organizational changes is assumed to be summarized as the parameter of the preference functions for the two divisions.

For simplicity, let's assume all preference functions, including the central unit, are exponential, and the parameters represented as $\lambda_1$, $\lambda_2$, and $\lambda_0$ respectively (the suffix 0 will always represent the central unit). In addition, for simplicity, $x_1$ and $x_2$ are assumed to be joint normally distributed, and $\mu_1$, $\mu_2$, $\sigma_1$, $\sigma_2$ and $\sigma_{12}$ are notations for the expectations, the standard deviations and the covariance of the distribution.

If we denote the return for the control unit by y, and the capital allocation ratios for two divisions by $\alpha_1$ and $\alpha_2$ ($\alpha_1 + \alpha_2 = 1$), then the relation $y = \alpha_1 x_1 + \alpha_2 x_2$ holds and the distribution of y will also be normal with the expectation $\mu_0$ and the standard deviation $\sigma_0$, where

$$\mu_0 = \alpha_1 \mu_1 + \alpha_2 \mu_2 \quad \text{and} \quad \sigma_0^2 = \alpha_1^2 \sigma_1^2 + \alpha_2^2 \sigma_2^2 + 2\alpha_1 \alpha_2 \sigma_{12}$$

In these assumptions, the two divisions attempt to mazimize their expected preferences respectively under various conditions. Let us assume the environmental conditions are as follows:

$$\sigma_i = k_i \mu_i^{Si} \quad ; \quad k_i > 0, \quad S_i \geqq 1 \qquad (1)$$

Therefore, the maximizing problem for each division would be expressed by the following Lagrangean problem given $\lambda_1$ and $\lambda_2$, or, $\max_{\mu_i, \sigma_i, \eta_i} \phi_2$

where $\eta_i$ are Lagrangean parameters and

$$\phi_i = \lambda_i \mu_i - \frac{\sigma_i^2}{2} + \eta_i (\sigma_i - k_i \mu_i^{Si}), \; i = 1, 2 \qquad (2)$$

The first order conditions to these problems give us the following solutions for $\mu_i$s and $\sigma_i$s,

$$\mu_i^* = \left(\frac{\lambda_i}{k_i^2 S_i}\right)^{\frac{1}{2S_i - 1}}$$

$$i = 1, 2 \qquad (3)$$

$$\sigma_i^* = \left(\frac{\lambda_i}{k_i^{\frac{1}{S_i}} S_i}\right)^{\frac{1}{2S_i - 1}}$$

Moreover, these solutions give us the following sensitivities of changes in the behavior of the two divisions as follows,

$$\frac{\partial \mu_i^*}{\partial \lambda_i} = \frac{1}{2S_i - 1}\left(\frac{1}{k_i^2 S_i}\right)^{\frac{1}{2S_i-1}} \lambda_i^{\frac{-2S_i+2}{2S_i-1}}$$

and $\qquad i = 1, 2 \qquad (4)$

$$\frac{\partial \sigma_i^*}{\partial \lambda_i} = \frac{S_i}{2S_i - 1}\left(\frac{1}{k_i^{\frac{1}{S_i}} S_i}\right)^{\frac{S_i}{2S_i-1}} \lambda_i^{\frac{-S_i-1}{2S_i-1}}$$

These equations might explain the summary effect of the various organizational changes on divisional behavior under environmental conditions. It might be interesting to note that signs of these quantities are always positive under our assumptions for values of $k_i$s and $s_i$s. In other words, to change the organizations in order to decrease the risk aversion always causes the division to increase the expected return, and, at the same time, increases the variance of the return. Another point to note is that if $s_i = 1$, then the decrease in the risk aversion will have a constant effect on divisional behavior.

Next, let's consider the program from the viewpoint of the central unit. It is natural for us to think that the central unit may be interested in exploiting divisional behavior patterns described above under their various environmental conditions. In doing so, we will assume that the central unit is able to manipulate parameters of divisional preference functions, in addition to capital allocation rates (i = 1, 2), and decision variables in the usual portfolio analysis setting. For the time being, assume this were in fact valid, and, for the sake of simplicity, optimal $\alpha_i$s would be attained at some value between 0 and 1. Under these assumptions, the problem of the central unit is to maximize $\phi_0$ with respect to $\lambda_1$, $\lambda_2$, $\alpha_1$, $\alpha_2$, and $\eta_0$, where

$$\phi_0 = (\lambda_0\mu_0 - \frac{\sigma_0^2}{2}) + \eta_0 (\Sigma\alpha_i - 1),$$

$$\mu_0 = \alpha_1\mu_1^* + \alpha_2\mu_2^*, \tag{5}$$

$$\sigma_0^2 = \sum_{i=1,\, j=1}^{2} \alpha_i\alpha_j\sigma_i^*\sigma_j^* r_{ij}$$

The last equation introduces a further assumption that the effect of divisional behavior on covariances would be such that the correlation coefficient between Division 1 and Division 2 would not change. This assumption might seem dubious, but, taken at least as the first approximation to reality. Again, the first order condition will lead us to the following key equation,

$$\mu_2^* \left( 1 - \frac{\frac{\partial\mu_2^*}{\partial\sigma_2} \Big/ \mu_2^*}{\frac{\partial\sigma_2^*}{\partial\lambda_2} \Big/ \sigma_2^*} \right) = \mu_1^* \left( 1 - \frac{\frac{\partial\mu_1^*}{\partial\lambda_1} \Big/ \mu_1^*}{\frac{\partial\sigma_1^*}{\partial\lambda_1} \Big/ \sigma_1^*} \right) \tag{6}$$

It might be thoughtful to show a reasonable behavioral pattern of the central unit, because this equation shows that the central unit should manipulate $\lambda_1$ and $\lambda_2$ in such a way that if the cross elasticity between $\mu_i$ and $\sigma_i$ should be equal, rates of return for both divisions should also be assigned to be equal.

In our model, the elasticities are simply reduced to $1/s_i$. Therefore, if $s_i$ is large (which means the environmental condition is more severe for the division i), then $\mu_i$ should be adjusted to become smaller, and vice versa.

Generally speaking, from this sort of equation we would be able to obtain expressions for $\alpha_i$s in terms of $\lambda_i$s. Furthermore, weight conditions for $\alpha_i$s would give us optimal $\alpha_i^*$s and $\lambda_i^*$s simultaneously, and, this process would be easily extended to the case where the central unit has n divisions.

In our model, we shall examine a few special cases. For example, if all $s_i$s are equal, it can be shown that

$$\lambda^*_k = \lambda_0 \sum_{i,j} \frac{k_k^2}{k_i k_j} r_{ij}^{-1}$$

and (7)

$$\alpha^*_k = \frac{\lambda_0}{\lambda^*_k} \sum_{i=1} \frac{k_k}{k_i} r_{ki}^{-1}$$

where $r_{ij}^{-1}$s are elements in the inverse of the correlation matrix. Especially for n = 2 optimal solutions are the following,

$$\lambda_1^* = \lambda_0 \frac{k_1^2}{k_2^2} \left[ 1 + \frac{\left(\frac{k_1}{k_2} - r\right)^2}{(1 - r^2)} \right],$$

and (8)

$$\lambda_2^* = \lambda_0 \left[ 1 + \frac{\left(\frac{k_2}{k_1} - r\right)}{(1 - r^2)} \right],$$

$$\alpha_1^* = \frac{\lambda_0}{\lambda_1^* (1-r^2)} \left[ 1 + \frac{k_1}{k_2} r \right],$$

$$\alpha_2^* = \frac{\lambda_0}{\lambda_2^* (1-r^2)} \left[ 1 + \frac{k_2}{k_1} r \right].$$

Moreover, if r = 0, solutions are simply to make

$$\lambda_1^* = \lambda_0\left(1 + \frac{k_1^2}{k_2^2}\right), \quad \lambda_2^* = \lambda_0\left(1 + \frac{k_2^2}{k_1^2}\right), \tag{9}$$

$$\alpha_1 = \frac{\lambda_0}{\lambda_1^*}, \quad \alpha_2^* = \frac{\lambda_0}{\lambda_2^*}$$

## 3. Analysis of Data

So far we have proposed a simple model based on various assumptions and examined some theoretical results. In doing so, we have neglected many aspects of reality. But, the validity of the assumptions should be examined at least, if possible. One possibility would be to examine the environmental conditions which the various firms are operating under.

First, we attempted to specify the environmental characteristics by computing the so-called "efficient boundaries" for various industries using statistics for the rate of net profit over total used capital of individual companies in Japan from 1968 to 1978. These boundaries are understood to represent the most efficient operational level in which an existing company in an industry could achieve through devoting all first-class resources in that industry.

Our model specification proposes the approximation of these boundaries by simple power functions. In order to do this, instead of calculating all points of the efficient boundary, we used the points of portfolio change as data and obtained a regression line. For instance, the following figures show such boundaries for machine and car industries with each k and s. They also show positions of the individual companies. For these industries, approximation is almost satisfactory, but, for some industries, i.e., electrical, we cannot obtain good approximations.

Figure 1. Efficient boundary for machine industry

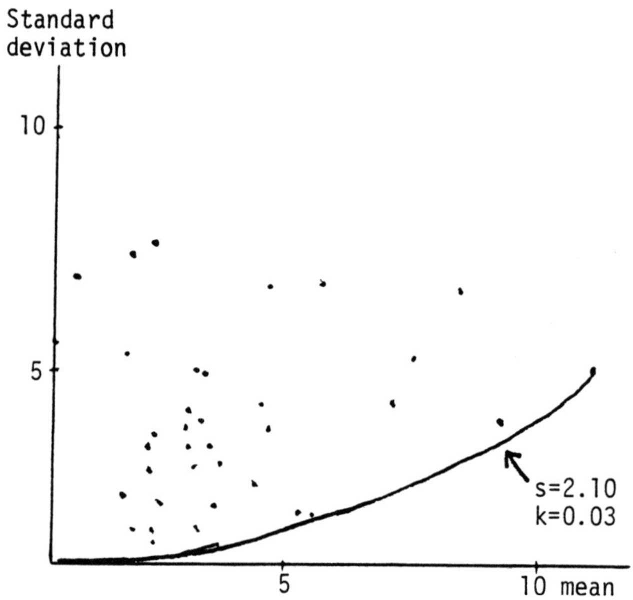


Figure 2. Efficient boundary for car industry

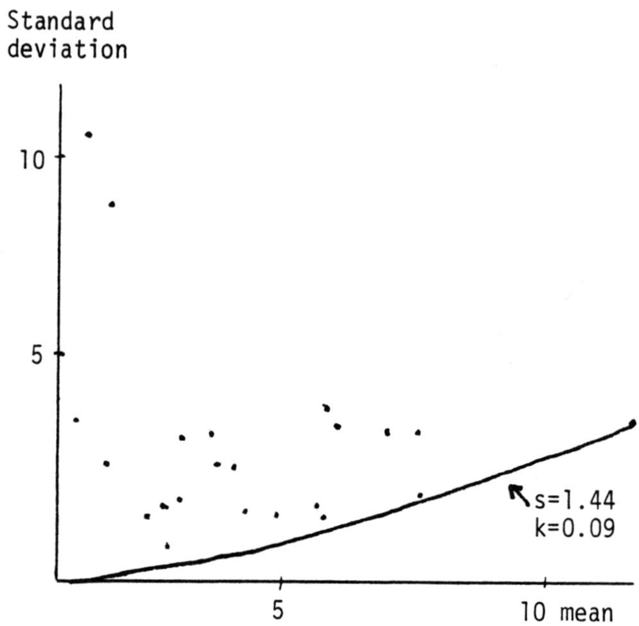

The expression (a) $\varepsilon_{ij} = \sigma_{ij}/k_i\mu_{ij}^{Si}$, or (b) $\varepsilon_{ij} = \sigma_{ij} - k_i\mu_{ij}^{Si}$ for company j in industry i could be regarded as a sort of distance from the efficient boundary to company j, and all companies with industry i could be classified according to the value $\varepsilon_{ij}$. If $\varepsilon_{ij}$ is large, it may cause difficulty to improve the operation of company j to the efficient boundary. Both expressions (a) and (b) were examined, and, as a result, we considered expression (b) which seemed to better explain the differences of the individual companies. The following tables show $\varepsilon_{ij}$ for some companies within the two industries shown above.

Table 1

$\varepsilon$ and $\lambda$ for Machine Industry

| Company | $\varepsilon$ | $\lambda$ |
|---|---|---|
| Brother Industries | 0.048 | 2.471 |
| Janome Sewing Machine | 0.234 | 0.321 |
| Kubota | 0.315 | 0.336 |
| Riccar Sewing Machine | 0.471 | 0.077 |
| Nippon Typewriter | 0.522 | 0.131 |
| National Cash Register | 0.638 | 1.297 |
| Amatsuji Steel Ball | 2.507 | 1.796 |

Table 2

$\varepsilon$ and $\lambda$ for Car Industry

| Company | $\varepsilon$ | $\lambda$ |
|---|---|---|
| Toyota Motor | 0.027 | 1.097 |
| Nippon Denso | 0.037 | 0.473 |
| Nissan Motor | 0.238 | 0.323 |
| Hino Motors | 0.389 | 0.218 |
| Honda Motor | 0.542 | 0.386 |
| Isuzu Motors | 2.016 | 0.128 |

In addition, it is desirable to show other characteristics of company j measuring the attitudes toward risk. In doing so, we should calculate $\lambda_{ij}$ using equations (3) and (b) in which $\sigma_i$, $\mu_i$ are replaced by $\sigma_{ij}$, $\mu_{ij}$. This measure gives us a tangent to the curve $\varepsilon_{ij} = \text{const.}$ at the point $(\mu_{ij}, \sigma_{ij})$. By these two measures, namely $\varepsilon_{ij}$ and $\lambda_{ij}$, we can characterize the companies more significantly. The tables above also include some $\lambda$s.

Although dubious assumptions have been made, the results were not as disappointing as expected, because after roughly classifying the firms within an industry, according to the scale of capital and the type of operation, the order of values for $\lambda$s does approximately correspond to the intuitive judgment concerning the order of attitudes toward risk which are assessed from the past behavior of the firms.

Another assumption which should be verified is the constancy of correlations. In doing so, we took several pairs of industries and calculated correlations between a firm in an industry and various firms in the same boundary for the other industry. The results are not as promising, and $\lambda$s seem to give some effects to correlations. Of course these effects are very different depending on the firms and/or industries examined. Therefore, in this respect, it is clear that our model should somehow be modified, but, at the present, we must wait and see future theoretical developments.

## 4. Discussion

As for the application of this model, the acquisition problem is most immediate and promising. Usually, the most important factors in the acquisition of other companies are the problems of management, especially how it should be adjusted for the company as a whole. This aspect could rarely be analytical and decisions of this sort are usually made by mere intuition. In this respect, although this is a very rough estimate, it seems to be helpful as a first approach in analyzing these kinds of problems.

Secondly, it is extremely difficult to persuade the lower levels to accept the target rate of return which is quite different from the recognition of the environment at the divisional level. The reason for this might again be due to the absence of relevant rationalization for the target. In regards to this, the above model might give some reasoning and somewhat reduce the burden of negotiations usually taken place among the central unit and its lower levels.

At this stage, it is appropriate to mention the most serious assumption in our model, that is, the feasibility of manipulating parameters of the preference functions. Thus, we would like to point out two possible interpretations. One is the change of divisional key personnel. The most powerful control means are often said to be in the allocation of human resources. However, the way of allocating such resources is rarely made explicit, except the physical or economic characteristics of human resources.

Therefore, the implication of our model is to measure the preference functions of the existing or available personnel and select combinations of them most closely "fitted" to the characteristics for various divisions. This might be useful, at least as a rough measure, for the central unit to control the hierarchical organization whenever surrounding uncertainties are great.

The other interpretation which is more indirect and has broader implications including the first would be to consider the parameters as summarizing effects of the underlying complex whose effects cannot be measured explicitly. In this case, we must choose between implicit and intuitive judgements based on usual personnel records and the judgement based on a rough but explicit measurement. We do believe, however, the latter judgement will contribute to the improvement of the former. Therefore, we should try both as much as possible, admitting that there is not only one method.

Although our empirical findings are far from comprehensive, we believe that they give prior knowledge about the feasibility of our model. And, this knowledge must be verified with additional microscopic data. For example, we would refine our intuitive judgement about the ranking of attitudes toward risk. For this purpose, we must check by collecting additional objective data.

In concluding our discussion, we would like to mention the possible extensions of our model. First, effects of information structure should be incorporated. Secondly, the relationship between $\lambda$s and feasible decisions should be further clarified. Thirdly, the other types of preference functions, for example, those of decreasing risk aversion and probability distribution such as the Pareto distribution should be explored. Fourth, the other types of environmental conditions should be examined further. Fifth, we neglected the cost aspect of the implementation of this model, and, thus, it should be taken into account. Finally, our model presented here might be rather expository in nature. However, the implications of our model seem to be broader. Therefore, other types of organizational settings other than portfolio analysis should be explored.

# DIRECT COSTING FOR PRICING CUSTOM-MADE PRODUCTS IN JAPAN'S INDUSTRIES

by Kengo Kobayashi

## Introduction

In Japan, the Cost Accounting Standards released by the Business Accounting Council of the Ministry of Finance is considered to have the opinion that direct costing concepts of net income and the practice of stating inventories at direct costs does not meet current accepted accounting standards for external reporting.

According to the Standards, it is required that when inventories are valued at direct costs for internal purposes, fixed overhead should be allocated to inventories and cost of sales figures at the end of each fiscal year.

The National Tax Administration Agency, in addition, usually rejects income statements prepared on a direct-cost basis. The difficulties of using direct costing for external reporting make many Japanese companies hesitate to change from absorption costing to directing costing. They don't like to get into trouble to adjust net income figures and inventories because they don't know exactly how to do this adjustment. Nothing has been stated by the Standards and the Agency regarding adjustment procedures, hitherto.

A tendency to accept relatively simple adjustment procedures for external reporting has been seen lately. For example, the Special Research Committee on the Cost Accounting Standards of the Japanese Accounting Association, including the Committee Chairman, Professor

Kiyoshi Okamoto, and the writer of this paper, recommended several adjustment procedures in a tentative statement of the Committee, which was presented at the annual conference of the Association in June, 1979.

Observing that almost all leading companies in Japan are separating fixed costs from variable costs for internal purposes, the acceptance practice will bring direct costing to use by a number of growing companies.

Another problem which is hindering the expansion of direct costing in Japan is that many company executives are suspicious of the usefulness of direct costing in pricing custom-made products. The Cost Accounting Standards also did not refer to the application of direct costing in custom-made product companies. The reason why no reference was made in the Standards was not explained. However, it is generally understood that the adjustment procedures approved implicitly by the Standards are not the allocation of fixed overhead to inventories and cost of sales figures by each sum total amount, but, by the assignment of fixed overhead to each order at the end of the fiscal year. It is easy to imagine that such a need for complicated procedures will discourage many companies from the application of direct costing even in its internal purposes. Here again, an acceptance of relatively simple adjustment procedures will eliminate the great obstacle of direct costing. But, there remains a problem of pricing these types of products. We will review this problem in some detail later.

## Product Pricing for Custom-Made Products

As in many other countries, companies differ greatly in regards to cost payments as a basis for pricing in Japan. Some companies adhere to it rigidly, others merely take the cost figures as a guide, selling as much as possible for it. In this paper we limit our problem to pricing custom-made products.

Determining product pricing for custom-made products is more difficult than for standardized products for three reasons.

First, because custom-made products are "made-to-order," a new price for each product must be given. There is no well-established market price to which the pricing manager can refer for guidance in setting the price. Under such circumstances, order costs receive more consideration in pricing than when standardized products are sold at the list price. Because the custom-made product has its own costs, cost estimation must be made for each order before pricing. The cost estimation for custom-made products has not been systemized in most companies in Japan and is still one of the most difficult problems for management within these companies.

Second, as stated in a management services technical study published by the AICPA, "Price is the most important method of competition in the manufacture of custom-made products; competing by a means of extremely effective distribution policies or through product differentiation is impossible because the physical characteristics and service requirements for the product are specified by the customer." (This is also true for Japan.)

Third, the fact that cost receives more consideration in pricing custom-made products does not mean that pricing always is practiced by applying a standard percentage margin on the costs of products. Custom-made product companies need to obtain enough volume of orders at an adequate price. Management must consider the volume that can be sold together with each product price received. Both of these factors affect the amount of profit.

Applying too high a margin percentage to costs for obtaining sufficient profit, the company will lose a substantial amount of backlog orders because of the elevated price and thus, the expected profit cannot be obtained. On the contrary, charging a lower margin percentage to costs, the company will obtain a sizeable amount of backlog orders. However, it must be noted that, in some cases, the company may not earn expected profits because of lower margins - even resulting in a loss.

Assuming that we can obtain and employ a standard percentage on cost, with which a satisfactory volume of orders will be received, the problem is not a difficult one to solve. But, in general, such a standard percentage cannot be employed. This difficulty is partly due to the fact that different bids or requests for quotation from potential customers in a certain period will accrue not simultaneously but in the course of time, and it will be impossible to select jobs in the order of their profitability. Management must decide whether to accept or reject each order at the time they take place. And, thereby, at the end of the period, sufficient volume and adequate profit must be realized.

Before direct costing had been well-acknowledged in Japan, many companies had used a custom-made product pricing formula called (in Japanese), "Juchu-Koshiki." This formula is a method of pricing policy which requires sufficient profit returns from each order. In the formula, when a competitive price is to be adjusted, the estimated full cost is multiplied by a desired percentage to obtain a quotation price. When the price is offered, a desired profit margin is deducted from that price, and an allowed full-cost for the order is computed. Then, the allowed cost is compared to the estimated cost. The decision to receive the order or not is made based on this comparison. As mentioned in the explanation of the formula, the order should be accepted only when the estimated cost does not exceed the allowed cost.

The desired profit or the desired percentage in this formula is derived from sources within various companies. In some companies, it is derived from their planned ratio of profit to sales in period profit planning, and in others, it is decided by the pricing manager based on his past experience.

It can be said that companies using this formula generally strive for a fair return which is expressed as a rate of the selling price or costs to produce and sell. But, as mentioned above, if the sales volume is insufficient because of over-pricing, expected periodic profit will not be realized, and, in some cases, fixed costs may not be fully covered. (This is illustrated in Figure 1 )

In this example, when periodic fixed costs amount to 5,600 yen by the accepted orders during the period, only 2,840 yen of the fixed costs is absorbed, and, the under-absorbed fixed costs in the period amount to 2,760 yen (5,600 - 2,840 = 2,760). Each of the orders accepted earns a desired margin percentage on costs, however, the accepted order volume is not sufficient to absorb all fixed costs.

When total volume of orders offered during the period are exactly sufficient to absorb all fixed costs, acceptance of all orders will yield profit amounting to 3,502 yen. The lack of sufficient order volume will make it more preferable to accept all orders than to adapt

Figure 1

Appreciation of Pricing Formula on a Full-Cost Basis

| Orders Offered | Estimated Cost | Desired Price* | Offered Price | Decision Made |
|---|---|---|---|---|
| A | 1,550 yen | 1,860 yen | 1,880 yen | Accepted |
| B | 3,865 | 4,638 | 4,210 | Rejected |
| C | 2,558 | 3,070 | 3,210 | Accepted |
| D | 3,255 | 3,906 | 3,910 | Accepted |
| E | 2,785 | 3,342 | 2,780 | Rejected |
| F | 1,690 | 2,028 | 2,040 | Accepted |
| G | 5,870 | 7,044 | 6,980 | Rejected |
| H | 4,235 | 5,082 | 4,300 | Accepted |
| Total during the period | 25,808 yen | | 29,310 yen | |
| Accepted | 13,288 yen | | 16,141 yen | |

Profit expected (16,141 yen - 13,288 yen) = 2,853 yen

*The desired margin percentage is assumed to be 20% of the estimated cost.

the pricing formula. But, we cannot make a decision whether to accept or reject each order at the time offered to obtain maximum profits on a full-cost basis.

It can be assumed that World War II created a stimulus toward using this formula as a basis for pricing. During the war, many companies had government cost-plus-fixed-fee contracts, and the guidelines of cost accounting released by the army and navy required full-cost basis. After the war, the Japanese economy expanded rapidly (except the Post War Era) until the Oil Crisis in 1973. It allowed management to give greater consideration to full costs in pricing their products by using this formula, thus, assuring total cost recovery when sufficient demand exists.

The business executive in Japan usually feels that laying-off employees in his company will bring discredit upon his management record, and, therefore, tries to maintain his employees even in the pitfalls of depression. For this purpose, the company is ready to accept the order which will not cover its full costs but its labor costs along with other variable costs. Under these circumstances, management has come to recognize that the pricing formula does not work adequately enough. They need a method to provide for a more flexible cost basis for pricing than the pricing formula, a method which will serve more adequately under varying economic conditions especially after the Oil Crisis. This leads them to pay attention to direct costing for pricing purposes.

## Direct Costing for Pricing Purposes

At present, some business executives question the applicability of direct costing as a basis for pricing custom-made products. An executive of a leading electrical manufacturing company in Japan, who is one of the well-known cost accounting experts, confessed his anxiety about the danger of pricing too low on a direct cost basis. He said that it would confront serious issues in business management when the marginal income of each order is conceived as profit in real means and the need for recovering fixed overhead is forgotten.

Another executive of a large machine manufacturing company told me that his company ceased to adapt direct costing for pricing because of requests for profit information of each order on a full-cost basis from the foreman level. They wanted to know whether or not the order they made brought any profit to their company. Therefore, in this company, the profit information of each order is provided through factory foremen to their subordinates.

This is not an unusual case for custom-made product industries. It is said that productivity and profitability of these industries are usually less than those of consumer products industries. This conception promotes and keeps the cost consciousness of all members of the company at high levels.

Another level of management function which requires full-cost information, as is the case with other countries, is the sales department. They want to be provided with this information because they will be able to set pricing on a simple and clear basis and sometimes be able to blame cost estimate groups of losing any order which was quoted too high to be accepted by the customer. For this reason, though it is an exceptional case, in certain companies cost information is not provided to the sales department; only the desired and minimum prices for each order.

There are several reasons why direct costing is mistrusted for pricing custom-made products. Among them, perhaps, we can point out is the lack of a fair knowledge of direct costing. First, however, I would like to refer to some characteristic features in Japan.

In Japanese companies, direct labor costs are considered to be fixed, because full-time employees are paid on a monthly basis and will usually not be laid-off. Management must exert all possible efforts to obtain sufficient business which justifies to pay labor costs for idle time. From this, all labor costs are classified as fixed costs in many companies. But, management must stress recovery of labor costs along with variable costs in product pricing. Labor costs are "out-of-the-pocket" costs and at the same time are fixed costs.

Therefore, it is not applicable that the short-run incremental costs of producing and selling a custom-made product can be estimated with this type of direct cost. Direct costs of a custom-made product cannot serve as a minimum value to judge whether or not a certain price will be acceptable. Companies need other minimum prices above their direct costs. However, at what margin of their direct costs becomes clearly acceptable is very difficult to compute with direct costing.

It is easy to criticize this classification of labor cost as fixed costs. There are four major criticisms of this classification. The first insists that because labor costs are out-of-the-pocket costs, labor costs should be covered by the price of the product and should be charged to product costs.

The second insists that excluding labor costs from inventory costs reduces the amount of the company's stated current assets excessively. It cannot be accepted as a sound valuation even for internal reporting.

The third criticism argues that labor costs may be fixed costs in short-term periods, but, in the long run, they will vary with no rehiring for the vacancies created by retired employees or, in the worst condition with lay-offs. But, in the last case, employees laid-off are sometimes paid lower wages. Therefore, labor costs will not decrease as much as assumed.

Fourth, labor costs are not absolute fixed costs, but, are semi-variable or semi-fixed costs. For example, labor costs are constant for a given range of activity which can be performed with current workers, and then increased at a higher activity level by overtime payments or labor costs for additionally employed workers.

Though these criticisms are not entirely appropriate, I do not intend to bring forth any counterargument in this paper. But, I would like to point out that classifying labor costs to fixed costs is preferred for cost-volume-profit relationship analysis and profit planning in those companies mentioned above. And, it cannot be denied that there is a danger of under-pricing custom-made products on a direct cost basis.

This danger comes from the application of the same pricing procedures in direct costing as in full-costing. The vital point to bear in mind is the difference in interpretation of margin above costs between these two pricing procedures. In full-costing, the margin of a certain product usually means the increment in profit of a period. In direct costing, the margin above direct costs does not mean profit but contribution to fixed costs and profit. This difference has not come to a full understanding yet.

In pricing custom-made products based on a direct cost basis, we have the same problem of obtaining sufficient volume of orders at an appropriate price, as in pricing based on a full-cost basis. This is illustrated in Figure 2.

In this example, assume that the periodic fixed costs amount to 5,600 yen as stated before. The estimated marginal income figure of the period will be 9,106 yen and the estimated profit figure is 3,506 yen. The order B, E, and G will also be accepted because none of their desired prices is in excess of their offered price and thus, they exceed their direct costs.

Assume that the appointed delivery dates of each order offered during the period are in their offered sequence and none of them can delay to the next period; another order that may be offered after order H in the period will be rejected because of no-slack facilities to produce, even if new orders may contribute greatly to profit. As suggested in the apprehensiveness of the executive above, there is a tendency to accept orders easily resulting in high activity without sufficient profit.

Further, several custom-made product companies in Japan emphasize elastic pricing policies rather than pricing each product on a rigid marginal analysis.

## Estimation of Sales

Estimating the sales amount for the coming year is difficult in custom-made product companies. In the long run, it is important to

Figure 2

Application of Pricing on Direct Cost Basis

| Orders Offered | Estimated Direct Costs | Desired Price* | Offered Price | Decision Made |
|---|---|---|---|---|
| A | 1,213 yen | 1,859 yen | 1,880 yen | Accepted |
| B | 3,025 | 4,637 | 4,210 | Accepted |
| C | 2,003 | 3,071 | 3,210 | Accepted |
| D | 2,550 | 3,909 | 3,910 | Accepted |
| E | 2,180 | 3,342 | 2,780 | Accepted |
| F | 1,323 | 2,028 | 2,040 | Accepted |
| G | 4,595 | 7,044 | 6,980 | Accepted |
| H | 3,315 | 5,082 | 4,300 | Accepted |
| Total | 20,204 yen | | 29,310 yen | |

*Desired price is computed by multiplying direct costs by the desired mark-up rate of 153.3%. This mark-up factor of 53.3% is derived from period planning.

cover all costs and provide a reasonable profit by the sales revenue. But, this does not mean that cost data should be provided by a full-cost basis in establishing long-run pricing policies. The estimation of sales over a long period is more difficult than for a short period. Consequently, even if prices of each product may cover its full costs, the sales acquired at the end of a long period may not be sufficient to cover all costs. The same feature as illustrated in Figure 1 can be seen. Sales is sufficient only when the activity performed is equal to or at least near to the selected activity standard for allocating overhead to products.

Hence, in establishing pricing policies for the long run, cost data provided by direct costing and planned margin can be as useful as cost data by absorption costing. Long-range pricing cannot exist where custom-made products are concerned. There are only long-range pricing policies which indicate some general rule or procedure of pricing each order. This rule or procedure can be expressed either on an absorption or on a direct costing basis.

In the short-run, because pricing policies must indicate some concrete plan for pricing, they must be flexible to various economic environments as mentioned earlier. For this reason, many companies that use pricing on a full-cost basis actually set some allowance range for flexibility in their pricing formula. This allowance range is usually expressed in terms of the percentage of the selling price or costs of the product.

By this allowance, the tendency to reject such orders that cannot cover total product costs but do cover out-of-the-pocket costs and result in profit increase would not be removed.

Pricing on a full-cost basis also fails to recognize that all orders are not able to realize the same rate of profit and fails to distinguish the cost volume and the facility utilization that generates profit. Custom-made products are in a wide variety of cost factors and machine allocation requirements.

Ideally speaking, flexible pricing policies should be given consideration at least to those three factors, that is, product-line profitability, cost component, and the facility used. Such flexible pricing will not be able to be performed with absorption costing but only with direct costing.

I do not know any example of using flexible pricing policies in which those three factors are under full consideration, but I can find several cases of considering one or two of the three factors. Some companies set their price-screening formula for evaluating the offered price, which computes a target price with multiplying direct costs by a desired mark-up factor. The desired mark-up factor is usually translated from the profit planning of a company.

In this procedure, planned profit figures or the planned rate of return on investment is assigned to territory or product lines, and target marginal income of each sales territory or product line is computed. This marginal income is combined with product sales estimated in each territory or product line.

The target marginal income rate is calculated by the total sales amount of each territory or product line. From the marginal income rate, the desired price for each custom order and/or desired pricing mark-up factor is computed. In some cases, assignable fixed costs are also charged to the territory or product lines, and the target contribution is computed.

However, the desired selling price calculated by the price-screening formula provides only a standard price that is used to compare with the offered price and is considered as a starting point for flexible pricing. Flexibility in pricing custom-made products to various management environments means capability of selecting one out of several pricing procedures according to the situation of obtaining backlog orders. The rigid pricing formula is not desirable for flexible pricing. In lieu of this, pricing should include the process of selecting alternative pricing formulas or guidelines on the basis of combining management strategy, internal cost and capital data, and external marketing information. Consequently, another approach for pricing custom-made products is provided to some companies by setting desired marginal income per machine hour or per direct labor hour.

In any event, pricing policies that are based on marginal income are assumed to provide a good pricing guide by giving several pricing methods in those companies. For example, direct costs plus labor costs will set a minimum price to sell its products, and, mark-up factors, expected marginal income per machine hour, and so forth, will determine the target price.

## Dual Standard Pricing

In another large electrical manufacturing company, flexible pricing policies appear in the form of dual standard pricing. This pricing method consists of two pricing standards; one is set as the minimum price and the other as the corporate goal price. The minimum price is usually not an out-of-the-pocket recovery price under which cash loss is sustained. It is the price necessary to recover cash costs as well as to contribute to fixed costs and net profit to a certain extent. To what extent the price intends to contribute to is determined flexibly by management with regard to the economic environment at that time. Then, minimum prices will change in accordance with current pricing policies of the company.

On the other hand, the corporate goal price will not change for a budgetary year except under extreme circumstances. It is the price that links together corporate net profit. The standard pricing form of this type can be seen in several companies. But, determining the dual standard form varies in its procedure.

## Conclusion

Before concluding this paper, it is appropriate to point out clearly that companies which are using direct costing for custom-made product pricing are a minority. It is more difficult to find companies which have some kind of sophisticated flexible pricing formula or standard. Further observations can be made about the reasons for it not being widely used for pricing purposes.

First, in some cases, it is conceived to be difficult to obtain cost and sales estimates accurately enough to obtain meaningful results by adapting sophisticated pricing policies.

Second, published literature in which pricing procedures for custom-made products are developed and explained properly are very few, so far, in Japan.

Third, some companies have their own knowledge on pricing custom-made products (through actual practice), but there are rare opportunities to exchange ideas with other companies. Because people do not shift their employment, especially in large companies in Japan, the exchange and extension of knowledge between companies is not as rapid as in other countries. There are wide varieties of accounting procedures for internal uses based on this fact. The examples referred to in this paper also do not describe the whole feature in practice of the problem in Japan.

In summary, the practical application of direct costing has greatly progressed in the use for internal purposes such as profit planning, cost control, and financial reports to management. But, in the applications to guide pricing custom-made products, direct costing is not widely used yet. Only a few companies use direct costing in their flexible pricing policies or in their dual standard pricing methods. Direct costing practice for custom-made product pricing is still in its infancy. However, in these few cases, we can find several characteristics of management in Japanese industries.

# IMPROVING FLEXIBLE BUDGET: CONSIDERATION OF MULTI COST-CAUSING FACTORS AND THEIR INTERDEPENDENCIES

By Tetsuo Kobayashi

It is well recognized that a flexible budget gives better information for planning and performance evaluation than a fixed budget.[1] But, regardless of the former's theoretical advantages, it is not widely used in practice. According to the latest empirical research in Japan, made by T. Yoshikawa, the overhead budgets were based on a flexible basis by only 23% of the firms which replied to the questionnaire, while 66% applied the fixed overhead budgets.[2]

Shortage of the compulsory control function may be one of the basic reasons why flexible budgets are not widely used.[3] Flexible budgets do not give in advance the specified level under which actual costs should be kept. Before the end of the period, most of the managers do not know exactly to which level of expenses their goal is to be applied; if they were to individually estimate the actual volume, the coordinated activities of the whole company could not be obtained.

---

[1]This is explained in many text books of budgeting and cost accounting. Especially, see Horngren (1977), Ch. 8,9, and 10, Welsch (1957), Ch. 8 and 9.

[2]Yoshikawa (1979).

[3]See, for example, Mizoguchi (1958).

However, this does not mean that a fixed budget is more valuable. Adjusting the budget to changing conditions per se is rational. The preferred action is to search for better methods for controlling activities under changing conditions rather than adhere to a fixed budget.

In this paper, we would not like to deal with such a problem. The purpose of this paper is to explain how a traditional fixed budget can be improved through better mapping of real cost behavior. This paper is concerned particularly with how to delineate the behavior of costs which depend on a variety of factors.

In the next section, we see that the traditional flexible budget does not give a good mapping. In Section 3, we present a budgeting model which seems to be more appropriate for delineating the dependencies of costs on multi-causing factors by applying the structure matrix developed by R. Franke.[4] The formal model will be followed by a numerical example in Section 4. Finally, in Section 5, several remarks will be given on the problems of an extension of flexible budgets coupled with a structure matrix.

## Section 2

In traditional flexible budgeting, each overhead cost is estimated for the various volumes which may be realized. Table 1 exhibits such a flexible budget. The behavior of each overhead cost is stated here in terms of direct labors hours ($h_1$). The unit variable cost is ¥460 per labor hour, and the total fixed cost is

---

[4]Franke (1972), (1975), and (1976).

¥4,320,000. They can be restated by the following linear equation:

$$y = 4{,}320{,}000 + 460\ h_1 \qquad (1)$$

This process produces two kinds of products, A & B, and the expected output consists of 1,500 units of product A and 1,000 units of product B. It is assumed that one unit of each product requires 2.7 hours of $h_1$ under the standard conditions. Then the expected hours of $h_1$ will be 6,750 hours. We obtained the standard overhead rate by dividing the total budget under $h_1$ of 6,750 by these hours, or ¥ 1,100 per hour of $h_1$.

Table 1

| $h_1$ : in hours | 5,400 | 6,075 | 6,750 | 7,425 | fixed | variable coefficients |
|---|---|---|---|---|---|---|
| Salaries | ¥ 585,000 | ¥ 585,000 | ¥ 585,000 | ¥ 585,000 | 585,000 | 0 |
| Wages | 1,805,000 | 1,940,000 | 2,075,000 | 2,210,000 | 725,000 | 200 |
| Energy costs | 2,614,000 | 2,789,500 | 2,965,000 | 3,140,500 | 1,210,000 | 260 |
| Depreciation | 1,800,000 | 1,800,000 | 1,800,000 | 1,800,000 | 1,800,000 | 0 |
| Total | 6,804,000 | 7,114,500 | 7,425,000 | 7,735,500 | 4,320,000 | 460 |

Expected labor hours (basic volume) : 6,750 standard overhead rate: 1,100 per hour.

Table 2

| | |
|---|---|
| Salaries | ¥ 590,000 |
| Wages | 2,262,000 |
| Energy costs | 2,920,000 |
| Depreciation | 1,800,000 |
| Total | ¥7,572,000 |

During the month, 1,200 units of product A and 1,100 units of product B were produced; we assume that there was no work in progress at the beginning and the end of the month. Actual labor time of $h_1$ was 6,600 hours and the actual overhead costs were shown in Table 2. Then, we have the underabsorbed overhead variance as follows:

$$7,572,000 - 1,100\ [2.7\ (1,200) + 2.7\ (1,100)] = 7,572,000 - 6,831,000 = ¥741,000.$$

According to one method of traditional analysis, this variance will be subdivided as follows:

1. Spending variance:

   actual overhead - allowance for actual labor hours =
   7,572,000 - [4,320,000 + 460 (6,600)] = ¥216,000 (unfavorable).

2. Efficiency variance:

   allowance for actual labor hours - allowance for standard labor hours =

   [4,320,000 + 460(6,600)] - [4,320,000 + 460 (2.7(1,200) + 2.7 (1,100))] = ¥179,400 (unfavorable).

3. Volume variance:

   allowance for standard labor hours - absorbed overhead =

   [4,320,000 + 460 (2.7 (1,200) + 2.7 (1,100))] - 6,831,000 = ¥345,600 (unfavorable).

The usefulness of this analysis relies on the reality or the plausibility of cost behaviors delineated in the flexible budget; these could be judged in the individual cases. But, there is one weakness in this approach of the traditional flexible budgeting. We can say that it represents the cost behavior in terms of only one factor, even in the cases where the costs depend on a variety of factors. This may reproduce the distorted cost behaviors.

For example, suppose it is estimated that the overhead costs depend not only on $h_1$ but also on another kind of direct labor time ($h_2$), lot numbers for each product ($k_A$ and $k_B$), machine hours ($m$) and the length of calendar time ($t$, here $t=1$) in the following manner:

$$S^e = 585{,}000t$$
$$W^e = 725{,}000t + 12{,}000k_A + 20{,}400k_B\ 96h_1 + 80h_2 + 48m \qquad (2)$$
$$Q^e = 1{,}210{,}000t + 15{,}000k_A + 9{,}840k_B + 80h_1 + 40h_2 + 600m$$
$$D^e + 1{,}800{,}000t$$

where $S^e$, $W^e$, $Q^e$, and $D^e$ are the estimated values of salaries, wages, energy costs and depreciation, respectively.

The cost behaviors shown in Table 1 or equation (1) will coincide with the behaviors stated by equation (2), if and only if the ratios of other factors to $h_1$ have always unique values, in this example, $h_2: h_1 = 0.58 : 1, k_A: h_1 = 1: 675$, $k_B : h_1 = 1: 675$, and $m: h_1 = 0.2: 1$. But, in other cases, the total costs will be different from that in Table 1, even if the value of $h_1$ is the same.

The necessity of linking flexible budgets with the regular cost accounting system is perhaps the most basic reason why only one factor should be selected in the traditional flexible budget. If we should take into account multi-factors explicitly, we will have different overhead rates conditioned by possible combinations of such factors; therefore, if the ratios of other factors to $h_1$ were different from that above, the overhead rate would take values other than ¥1,100, even in the case; $h_1 = 6{,}750$ hours.

Then we will have a number of standard product costs for each product. But, this is not conventional. Thus, according to the traditional method, the fixed combinations of causing factors are predetermined so that one may obtain a single overhead rate.

But this makes the flexible budget inflexible. The cost information based on the predetermined fixed combinations of causing factors is not relevant to decision makers who will determine the combinations of these factors. Furthermore, the determined plans should be modified under changing conditions. The traditional approach neglects these requirements, and the traditional flexible budget is not flexible on this point. We can say that it is not impossible to develop a flexible budget apart from the thesis of product costing. It is not only possible but also desirable. We have new methods for improving flexible budgets by doing so. In the next section, we present a model of budgeting system which delineates the various possible dependencies of costs on their causing factors and the interdependencies of these factors.

## Section 3

In finding and delineating cost behaviors, it is normally desirable to differentiate the price ingredients from the quantity ingredients. But, for convenience, we treat the values as if the prices are constant.

If we find that the overhead costs vary directly depending on a number of the causing factors, we write such direct relationships in the following manner:

$$y_i = c_{i1}z_1 + c_{i2}z_2 + \ldots\ldots + c_{im}z_m \quad i = 1,\ldots,n \tag{3}$$

where $y_i$ is the value of cost item i in the period.

$z_1, z_2, \ldots, z_m$ are the values of cost causing factors in the period.

$c_{i1}, c_{i2}, \ldots, c_{im}$ are the coefficients which represent the dependencies of cost i on the causing factors,

or,

$$Y = CZ \tag{4}$$

where

$$Y = \begin{bmatrix} y_1 \\ y_2 \\ \vdots \\ y_n \end{bmatrix}, \quad Z = \begin{bmatrix} z_1 \\ z_2 \\ \vdots \\ z_n \end{bmatrix}, \quad C = \begin{bmatrix} c_{11} & c_{12} & \cdots & c_{1m} \\ c_{21} & c_{22} & \cdots & c_{2m} \\ \cdots & \cdots & \cdots & \cdots \\ c_{n1} & c_{n2} & \cdots & c_{nm} \end{bmatrix}$$

The causing factors are not necessarily independent from each other. In the example in Section 2, we may find that machine hours depend on the lot numbers and the direct labor hours. Such interdependencies may be better predicted.

We then divide the overhead vector Y into two column vectors, $Y_1$ and $Y_2$, while subdividing the causing factors vector Z into three column vectors, $z_1$, $z_2$, and $z_3$. Assume the following interdependencies exist between them: the values of the first group of overhead depend directly on the first and second groups of the causing factors, and the values of the second group of overhead depend directly on the second and third groups of causing factors, while the values of the second group of causing factors depend directly on the first group of causing factors, and the values of the third group of causing factors depend directly on the second group of causing factors. Then, we can approximate these interdependencies with the following equations, assuming there are linear relationships.

$$\begin{aligned} Z_2 &= R_{21}Z_1 \\ Z_3 &= R_{32}Z_2 \\ Y_1 &= C_{11}Z_1 + C_{12}Z_2 \\ Y_2 &= C_{22}Z_2 + C_{23}Z_3 \end{aligned} \tag{5}$$

where

$$Y = (Y_1 \ Y_2)^T$$
$$Z = (Z_1 \ Z_2 \ Z_3)^T$$

R(s): denotes the matrix of the coefficients which represent the interdependencies between the causing factors.

C(s): denotes the sub-matrix of the cost coefficient matrix.

According to Franke's formula,[5] we can present these relationships as shown in Table 3. Here, the oblique lines mean the diagonal unit matrices multipled by -1; thus, we read the first row as, $R_{21}Z_1 - EZ_2 = 0$.

Table 3

| | Cost-determining variables | | |
|---|---|---|---|
| | primary | secondary | |
| | $Z_1$ | $Z_2$ | $Z_3$ |
| $Z_2$ | $R_{21}$ | | |
| $Z_3$ | | $R_{32}$ | |
| $Y_1$ | $C_{11}$ | $C_{12}$ | |
| $Y_2$ | | $C_{22}$ | $C_{23}$ |

Noting the interdependencies between the causing or determining factors, we can eliminate some causing variables. In the above example, $Z_3$ and $Z_2$ can be eliminated, because $Z_3$ is determined by $Z_2$, and $Z_2$ is determined by $Z_1$. That is,

---

[5]Franke [1976].

$$Y = \begin{bmatrix} C_{11} & C_{12} & 0 \\ 0 & C_{22} & C_{23} \end{bmatrix} \begin{bmatrix} E & 0 & 0 \\ R_{21} & 0 & 0 \\ 0 & R_{32} & 0 \end{bmatrix} \begin{bmatrix} Z_1 \\ Z_2 \\ Z_3 \end{bmatrix}$$

$$= \begin{bmatrix} C_{11}Z_1 & + & C_{12}R_{21}Z_1 \\ C_{22}R_{21}Z_1 & + & C_{23}R_{32}Z_2 \end{bmatrix}$$

Since $Z_2 = R_{21}Z_1$

$$Y = \begin{bmatrix} (\ C_{11} & + & C_{12}R_{21} & )\ Z_1 \\ (\ C_{22}R_{21} & + & C_{23}R_{32}R_{21} & )\ Z_1 \end{bmatrix} \tag{6}$$

This reduced matrix is exhibited in Table 4.

Table 4

| | $Z_1$ |
|---|---|
| $Y_1$ | $C_{11} + C_{12}\ R_{21}$ |
| $Y_2$ | $C_{22}\ R_{21} + C_{23}\ R_{32}\ R_{21}$ |

Here, $Z_1$ is the set of exogenous variables which consist of the decision variables and the environmental variables. These variables are called primary causing or determining factors. On the other hand, $Z_2$ and $Z_3$ are secondary factors which are determined by the primary factors.

Using the reduced matrix is appropriate for various decision-making and product costing, because we can easily predict all the impacts of the changes of primary causing factors with it, including direct consequences. But, for controlling, it is necessary to keep the original structure matrix, because the direct relationships of costs with their causing factors and the interdependencies between the causing factors should be controlled in the operation process. Furthermore, we can determine the controllable and uncontrollable variances, taking the functional relationships in the original structure matrix into consideration, as we will see in a numerical example of the next section.

As for product costing, note that there exists not only the costs depending on the output of the products but also the costs depending on other primary causing factors. In order to apply the latter costs to the product unit, we need to assume specified relationships between production quantities and other primary factors. But, this assumption should be made outside of the model of the flexible budgeting system. At most, we can make the allocation after the values of the primary factors have been determined by a production plan. The determined value of the product cost reflects only one possibility under a variety of possible combinations of the primary factors. If the cost variances were determined in a cost accounting system combined with product costing, the restricted statements should be replenished by taking into consideration the possible relationships shown in the original structure matrix. This will also be seen in the example of the next section.

## Section 4

In this section, we illustrate a simple numerical example where the flexible budget based on the structure matrix is developed and applied to performance evaluation. We use here again the same example presented in Section 2, but additional detailed activities are introduced.

In the process of this example, two kinds of products are produced. We denote the output with $x_A$ and $x_B$. Two kinds of direct labor time are necessary to produce these products. It is estimated that 2.7

hours of the first kind of labor will be required for each unit of both products, and 1.35 hours and 1.89 hours of another kind of labor are required for each unit of the products, respectively. Hence, these estimated direct labor hours are as follows:

$$h_1 = 2.7x_A + 2.7x_B \text{ and } h_2 = 1.35x_A + 1.89x_B$$

Both products are produced in lots, and we assume that the lot numbers in a period are determined by the line manager. We denote the lot numbers for both products as $k_A$ and $k_B$. Finally, one kind of machine is used for producing both products. It is estimated that the machine hours (m) increase by 0.15 hour per hour of the first kind of direct labor and 0.1 hour per hour of another kind of labor, respectively, while they decrease by 3 hours per lot of product A and 2.4 hours per lot of product B, respectively. On the other hand, it is estimated that each class of overhead varies depending directly on these causing factors in the manner assumed in equations (2) of Section 2.

Thus, we have five categories of causing factors, that is, the length of calendar time, the lot numbers, the output quantities, the direct labor hours and the machine hours. We denote these causing factors with the following column vectors:

$$T = \begin{bmatrix} t \end{bmatrix}, \ K = \begin{bmatrix} k_A \\ k_B \end{bmatrix}, \ X = \begin{bmatrix} x_A \\ x_B \end{bmatrix}, \ H = \begin{bmatrix} h_1 \\ h_2 \end{bmatrix}, \ \text{and } M = \begin{bmatrix} m \end{bmatrix}.$$

Under the causing factors, T, K, and X are the sets of primary factors. T is given here as T = t = 1. The output quantities are assumed to be determined by the production planning for the whole company; then, X is a set of uncontrollable variables for the process manager. The lot numbers in K are assumed to be partly controlled by the process manager, since we assume that they will be determined under his judgement. Other variables in H and M are secondary causing factors.

Period overhead will also be written in a column vector:

$$Y = \begin{bmatrix} S & W & Q & D \end{bmatrix}^T.$$

Then, we have the structure matrix exhibited in Table 5 and its reduced form in Table 6.

Table 5

| | primary causing factors | | | | | secondary causing factors | | |
|---|---|---|---|---|---|---|---|---|
| | T | K | | X | | H | | M |
| H | | | | 2.7<br>1.35 | 2.7<br>1.89 | | | |
| M | | -3 | -2.4 | | | 0.15 | 0.1 | |
| S | 585,000 | | | | | | | |
| W | 725,000 | 12,000 | 20,400 | | | 96 | 80 | 48 |
| Q | 1,210,000 | 15,000 | 9,840 | | | 80 | 40 | 600 |
| D | 1,800,000 | | | | | | | |

Table 6

| | T | K | | X | |
|---|---|---|---|---|---|
| S | 585,000 | | | | |
| W | 725,000 | 11,856 | 20,284.8 | 393.12 | 438.912 |
| Q | 1,210,000 | 13,200 | 8,400 | 594 | 648 |
| D | 1,800,000 | | | | |

Specifically, we denote sub-matrices which contain the estimated coefficients, as follows:

$$R^e_{HX} = \begin{bmatrix} 2.7 & 2.7 \\ 1.35 & 1.89 \end{bmatrix}, \quad R^e_{MK} = \begin{bmatrix} -3 & -2.4 \end{bmatrix}, \quad R^e_{MH} = \begin{bmatrix} 0.15 & o.1 \end{bmatrix},$$

$$C^e = \begin{bmatrix} 585{,}000 & 0 & 0 & 0 & 0 & 0 \\ 725{,}000 & 12{,}000 & 20{,}400 & 96 & 80 & 48 \\ 1{,}210{,}000 & 15{,}000 & 9{,}840 & 80 & 40 & 600 \\ 1{,}800{,}000 & 0 & 0 & 0 & 0 & 0 \end{bmatrix} \text{ and}$$

$$\underline{C}^e = \begin{bmatrix} 585{,}000 & 0 & 0 & 0 & 0 \\ 725{,}000 & 11{,}856 & 20{,}284.8 & 393.12 & 438.912 \\ 1{,}210{,}000 & 13{,}200 & 8{,}400 & 594 & 648 \\ 1{,}800{,}000 & 0 & 0 & 0 & 0 \end{bmatrix}$$

From these matrices, we can predict how the overhead costs vary depending directly and indirectly on the causing factors. For example, from the reduced matrix in Table 6, it can be seen that a change in the lot number for product A by 1 leads to the change of ¥ 11,856 in wages and that of ¥ 13,200 in energy costs. Similarly, the increase of output B by one unit leads to the increase of ¥ 393.12

in wages and that of ¥ 594 in energy costs. Such information is useful for decision making. But, in the following, we show the use of the original structure matrix rather than the reduced matrix for the analysis of cost variances, although the reduced matrix is partially used in such analysis, also.

Now, the budgeted output quantities and the predetermined lot numbers are assumed to be:

$$X^e = \begin{bmatrix} 1,500 \\ 1,000 \end{bmatrix} \quad \text{and} \quad K^e = \begin{bmatrix} 10 \\ 10 \end{bmatrix}$$

From these, the estimated values of the secondary causing factors will be calculated as follows:

$$H^e = R^e_{HX} \cdot X^e = \begin{bmatrix} 6,750 \\ 3,915 \end{bmatrix} \quad \text{and} \quad M^e = R^e_{MK} \cdot K^e + R^e_{MH} \cdot H^e = 1,350.$$

Or, we have the vector of the estimated causing factors:

$$Z^e = [\ 1 \quad 10 \quad 10 \quad 6,750 \quad 3,915 \quad 1,350]^T .$$

Then, the budgeted overhead costs for the production plan are:

$$Y^e = C^e Z^e = \begin{bmatrix} S^e \\ W^e \\ Q^e \\ D^e \end{bmatrix} = \begin{bmatrix} 585,000 \\ 2,075,000 \\ 2,965,000 \\ 1,800,000 \end{bmatrix}$$

or,

$$Y^e = \underline{C}^e \begin{bmatrix} T \\ K^e \\ X^e \end{bmatrix}$$

At the end of the period, the actual values of the overhead were observed as shown in Table 2 of Section 2. The observed values of the causing factors were:

$$X^o = \begin{bmatrix} 1,200 \\ 1,000 \end{bmatrix}, \quad K^o = \begin{bmatrix} 9 \\ 11 \end{bmatrix}, \quad H^o = \begin{bmatrix} 6,600 \\ 3,520 \end{bmatrix} \text{ and } M^o = m^o = 1,252.$$

As a result, we have the cost variances between the observed values and the budgeted values in the production plan as follows:

$$\Delta Y = Y^o - Y^e = \begin{bmatrix} \Delta S \\ \Delta W \\ \Delta Q \\ \Delta D \end{bmatrix} = \begin{bmatrix} 5,000 \\ 187,000 \\ -45,000 \\ 0 \end{bmatrix}$$

where positive value means unfavorable variances and negative value means favorable variances.

Using the matrices given above, these variances will be subdivided into a number of sub-variances which suggest the possible causes and the controllabilities.

1. Variances caused by the lot numbers

$$\Delta Y_k = \underline{C}^e \begin{bmatrix} 0 \\ K^o - K^e \\ 0 \end{bmatrix} = \underline{C}^e \begin{bmatrix} 0 \\ 9 - 10 \\ 11 - 10 \\ 0 \\ 0 \end{bmatrix} = \begin{bmatrix} 0 \\ 8,428.8 \\ -4,800 \\ 0 \end{bmatrix}$$

or,

$$\Delta Y_k = c^e \begin{bmatrix} 0 \\ K^o - K^e \\ 0 \\ M|[K^o, H^e] - M^e \end{bmatrix} = c^e \begin{bmatrix} 0 \\ 9 - 10 \\ 11 - 10 \\ 0 \\ 0 \\ 1,350.6 - 1,350 \end{bmatrix}$$

where $M\,|[K^o, H^e] = R^e_{MK}\, K^o + R^e_{MH}\, H^e = 1,350.6$

2. Variances caused by the output quantities

$$\Delta Y_X = \underline{c}^e \begin{bmatrix} 0 \\ 0 \\ X^o - X^e \end{bmatrix} = \underline{c}^e \begin{bmatrix} 0 \\ 0 \\ 0 \\ 1,200 - 1,500 \\ 1,100 - 1,000 \end{bmatrix} = \begin{bmatrix} 0 \\ -74,044.8 \\ -113,400 \\ 0 \end{bmatrix}$$

or,

$$\Delta Y_X = c^e \begin{bmatrix} 0 \\ 0 \\ H|[X^o] - H^e \\ M|[K^e, X^o] - M^e \end{bmatrix} = c^e \begin{bmatrix} 0 \\ 0 \\ 0 \\ 6,210 - 6,750 \\ 3,699 - 3,915 \\ 1,247.4 - 1,350 \end{bmatrix}$$

where $H\,|[X^o] = R^e_{HX}\, X^o = \begin{bmatrix} 6,210 \\ 3,699 \end{bmatrix}$

$$M|[K^e, X^o] = R^e_{MK}\, K^e + R^e_{MH}\, R^e_{HX}\, X^o = 1,247.4$$

3. Variances caused by the direct labor hours adjusted for the output quantities.

$$\Delta Y_H = C^e \begin{bmatrix} 0 \\ 0 \\ H^o - H \mid [x^o] \\ M \mid [K^o, H^o] - M \mid [k^o, x^o] \end{bmatrix} = C^e \begin{bmatrix} 0 \\ 0 \\ 0 \\ 6{,}600 - 6{,}210 \\ 3{,}520 - 3{,}699 \\ 1{,}288.6 - 1{,}248 \end{bmatrix} = \begin{bmatrix} 0 \\ 25{,}068.8 \\ 48{,}400 \\ 0 \end{bmatrix}$$

$$\text{where } M \mid [K^o, H^o] = R^e_{MK} K^o + R^e_{MH} H^o = 1{,}288.6$$

$$M \mid [K^o, X^o] = R^e_{MK} K^o + R^e_{MH} R^e_{HX} X^o = 1{,}248$$

4. Variances caused by the machine hours adjusted for the lot numbers and the labor hours

$$\Delta Y_M = C^e \begin{bmatrix} 0 \\ 0 \\ 0 \\ M^o - M \mid [K^o, H^o] \end{bmatrix} = C^e \begin{bmatrix} 0 \\ 0 \\ 0 \\ 0 \\ 0 \\ 1{,}252 - 1{,}288.6 \end{bmatrix} = \begin{bmatrix} 0 \\ -1{,}756.8 \\ -21{,}960 \\ 0 \end{bmatrix}$$

5. Residual variances

$$\Delta Y_r = (Y^o - Y^e) - (\Delta Y_K + \Delta Y_X + \Delta Y_H + \Delta Y_M) = \begin{bmatrix} 5{,}000 \\ 229{,}304 \\ 46{,}760 \\ 0 \end{bmatrix}$$

$\Delta Y_k$ does not immediately mean the judgement of the process manager was right or wrong. It gives the starting point for further analysis of his decision under the changed output quantities. In this example, $\Delta Y_X$ is thought to be uncontrollable variances for him. On the other hand, $\Delta Y_H$ and $\Delta Y_M$ reflect the efficiencies of this process. Finally $\Delta Y_r$ contains not only the spending variances but also the variances caused by the error of predicting or measuring all the coefficients in the matrices. If possible, it is useful to isolate the latter variances from $\Delta Y_r$. But, this isolating presupposes that the true values of coefficients are known.

In the above, we have analyzed the differences between the observed costs and the budgeted costs in the primary production plan. This seems to be more valuable for budgetary control.[6] But, we can also consider the case where the cost variances are calculated in the cost accounting system coupled with the product costing. Under the principle of absorption costing, all overhead costs should be applied to product units. Therefore, we calculate the overhead rate through dividing the budgeted overhead in the primary production plan by the direct labor hours of $h_1$:

$$\boldsymbol{\theta} = \frac{C^e\ Z^e}{6{,}750} = \begin{bmatrix} \theta\ S \\ \theta\ W \\ \theta\ Q \\ \theta\ D \end{bmatrix} = \begin{bmatrix} 86.7 \\ 307.4 \\ 439.3 \\ 266.6 \end{bmatrix}, \text{ or } [\ 1\ 1\ 1\ 1\ ]\ \boldsymbol{\theta} = ¥1{,}100.$$

---

[6]Horngren [1974], pp. 312-315.

Applying this overhead rate, we have the absorbed overhead of ¥6,831,000 and the cost variances of ¥741,000 (underabsorbed). This result is the same as in Section 2. However, here we subdivide these cost variances into three types of variances as follows:

1. Spending variances

$$\Delta Y_1 = Y^o - c^e Z^o = \begin{bmatrix} 5,000 \\ 229,304 \\ 46,760 \\ 0 \end{bmatrix}$$

2. Efficiency variances

$$\Delta Y_2 = c^e \begin{bmatrix} 0 \\ 0 \\ H^o - H|[X^o] \\ M^o - M|[K^o, X^o] \end{bmatrix} = c^e \begin{bmatrix} 0 \\ 0 \\ 0 \\ 6,600 - 6,210 \\ 3,520 - 3,699 \\ 1,252 - 1,248 \end{bmatrix} - \begin{bmatrix} 0 \\ 23,312 \\ 26,440 \\ 0 \end{bmatrix}$$

These variances might be further divided into $Y_H$ and $Y_M$, since

$M^o - M|[K^o, X^o] = (M|[K^o, H^o] - M|[K^o, X^o]) + (M^o - M|[X^o, H^o])$. That is

$$\Delta Y_2 = \Delta Y_H + \Delta Y_M = \begin{bmatrix} 0 \\ 25,068.8 \\ 48,400 \\ 0 \end{bmatrix} + \begin{bmatrix} 0 \\ -\ 1,756.8 \\ -\ 21,960 \\ 0 \end{bmatrix}$$

3. Volume variances

$$\Delta Y_3 = c^e \begin{bmatrix} T \\ K^o \\ H|[X^o] \\ M|[K^o, X^o] \end{bmatrix} - \begin{bmatrix} \theta_S \cdot h_1|[X^o] \\ \theta_W \cdot h_1|[X^o] \\ \theta_Q \cdot h_1|[X^o] \\ \theta_D \cdot h_1|[X^o] \end{bmatrix} = \begin{bmatrix} 46,593 \\ 100,430 \\ 118,747 \\ 144,414 \end{bmatrix}$$

The spending variances and two sets of the efficiency variances are the same as the variances in the analysis above, although the volume variances are not apparent. The summarized results are exhibited in Table 7. Note that the results of the traditional analysis are not the same as that of the second analysis in this section; in the former, the relationships shown in the structure matrix are not adequately considered.

Table 7

<table>
<tr><td rowspan="2">Variances from the budgeted overhead in primary production plan</td><td colspan="3">Variances from the absorbed overhead</td></tr>
<tr><td colspan="2">Analysis based on the structure matrix</td><td>Traditional analysis</td></tr>
<tr><td>Lot number variance<br>($E\Delta Y_K$) ¥ 3,628.8</td><td colspan="2"></td><td></td></tr>
<tr><td>Output variance<br>($E\Delta Y_X$) ¥-187,444.8</td><td colspan="2"></td><td></td></tr>
<tr><td>Residual variance<br>($E\Delta Y_r$) ¥ 281,064</td><td colspan="2">Spending variance<br>($E\ Y_1$) ¥ 281,064</td><td>Spending variance<br>¥ 216,000</td></tr>
<tr><td>Labor hour variance<br>($E\Delta Y_H$) ¥ 73,468.8</td><td>Labor hour var.($E\ Y_H$)<br>¥73,468.8</td><td rowspan="2">Efficiency variance<br>($E\ Y_2$)<br>¥49,752</td><td rowspan="2">Efficiency variance<br>¥ 179,400</td></tr>
<tr><td>Machine hour variance<br>($E\Delta Y_M$) ¥ -23,716.8</td><td>Machine hour var.($E\ Y_M$)<br>¥-23,716.8</td></tr>
<tr><td></td><td colspan="2">Volume variance<br>($E\ Y_3$)<br>¥ 410,184</td><td>Volume variance<br>¥ 345,600</td></tr>
<tr><td>Total ¥ 147,000</td><td colspan="2">Total ¥ 741,000</td><td>Total ¥ 741,000</td></tr>
</table>

E means row unit vector. Positive values: unfavorable, negative: favorable.

We have explained an extension of flexible budgets coupled with a structure matrix. But, in practice, some problems may exist in applying this method.

First, we may have more expenses of budgeting or of measuring the activities contained in the budget system. Therefore, we must introduce this method under the consideration of cost-benefit relationships. However, we may say that one positive feature of this method lies in its structural flexibility. If the detailed structure matrix is too costly, a more simplified structure matrix can be used. In doing so, this method and the system could easily be adapted to individual cases.

Second, there are some statistical problems to be resolved for estimating the functional relationships contained in the structure matrix. Some relationships might be determined under the technological or engineering standpoint, but there are also the relationships which should be determined by applying some statistical methods, especially multi-regression analysis. Such methods have a tendency toward a wide-use in the accounting field also, but there exists some difficulties to overcome; for example, multicollinearity, serial correlation, and so forth.[7]

---

[7]These problems are mentioned, for example by Benston [1966]. He maintains introducing multi-regression techniques into accounting measurements including flexible budgeting, also.

Specifically, in our model, we must apply an indirect-least-squares method, especially a two-stage least squares method rather than a direct least squares method for determining the coefficients in the original structure matrix. The functional relationships, for example, between $Y_1$, $Z_1$, and $Z_2$ in equations (5) of Section 3 can be better represented in the following form, considering the disturbances $U_1$ and $U_2$ that are assumed to have means of zero with constant variances:

$$Y_1 = C_{11} Z_1 + C_{12} Z_2 + U_1 \tag{7}$$

$$Z_2 = R_{21} Z_1 + U_2 \tag{8}$$

However, in this case, $U_1$ is apparently not uncorrelated with $Z_1$ and $Z_2$. Therefore, applying least squares method directly to (7) is unreasonable.[8] We must apply the least squares method to the following reduced equation derived from (7) and (8):

$$Y_1 = C_{11} Z_1 + C_{12} (R_{21} Z_1 + U_2) = (C_{11} + C_{12} R_{21}) Z_1 + C_{12} U_2 \tag{9}$$

We know that the estimates of the coefficients cannot be statistically determined in the case of simultaneous equation systems even by a two-stage least squares method if we have an underidentified structural relation. Fortunately, the equation system as in (7) and (8) is able to be represented by a triangular matrix having all zero elements above the diagonal, that is:

---

[8]See, for example, Johnston [1972], Ch. 12 and Ch. 13, and Monden-Kato [1979].

$$\begin{bmatrix} 0 & 0 & 0 \\ R_{21} & -E & 0 \\ C_{11} & C_{12} & -E \end{bmatrix} \begin{bmatrix} Z_1 \\ Z_2 \\ Y_1 \end{bmatrix} \begin{matrix} = \\ = \\ = \end{matrix} \begin{bmatrix} 0 \\ -U_2 \\ -U_1 \end{bmatrix} \tag{10}$$

Then, we have a recursive system, where all the equations are known to be identifiable. But, it is assumed here that a certain causal sequence is known. If such a causal sequence is not known, we have no recursive systems. A causal ordering is a problem requiring some managerial discretions.[9]

Finally, it is valuable to apply this approach to the whole cost accounting system, because in the computerized information systems, finding and keeping the possible relationships of the firm is the first step for building a data base, from which various useful data for decision making and control are supplied. Such a system is already employed in an iron and steel company,[10] and some Japanese companies will also try to initiate it. But, in this paper we have just explained one application of this approach for overhead control.

---

[9]Danielson [1963] applies the causal ordering to measurement and analysis of standard direct costs.

[10]ter Schüren - Wartmann [1976] and Walter [1977].

## References


1. Benston, G.J., "Multiple Regression Analysis of Cost Behavior," The Accounting Review, Oct. 1966, pp. 657-672.

2. Danielsson, A., "On Measurement and Analysis of Standard Costs," The Business Research Institute at the Stockholm School of Economics, 1963.

3. Franke, R., Betriebsmodelle, Bertelsmann Universitätsverlag, 1972.

4. ------------, "A Process Model for Costing," Management Accounting, Jan. 1975.

5. ------------, "Costing with Matrix Analysis," Management Accounting, Apr. 1976.

6. Horngren, C.T., Cost Accounting: A Managerial Emphasis, 4th ed., Prentice-Hall, 1977.

7. Johnston, J., Econometric Methods, 2nd ed., McGraw-Hill Book Co., 1972.

8. Mizoguchi, K., "Overhead Cost Control," Accounting (Kaikei), July 1958.

9. Monden, Y., and Y. Kato, "Matrix Costing: Determination of Its Coefficients and Variance Analysis," Accounting (Kigyokaikei), Nov. 1979.

10. ter Schüren, H., und R. Wartmann, "Richtkosten - und Planungsrechnung mit Matrizen für den Hochofenbereich eines gemischten Hüttenwerkes," in: Neuere Entwicklung in der Kostenrechnung (1), Bd. 21, edited by H. Jacob, Gabler Verlag, 1976, pp. 142-162.

11. Walter, K.D., Gestaltung und Verwirklichung linearer Modelle zur Unternehmung, Studienverlag Dr. N. Brockmeiyer, 1977.

12. Welsch, G.A., Budgeting: Profit-Planning and Control, Prentice-Hall, 1957.

13. Yoshikawa, T., "Investigation of Cost Accounting Practice (in Japan)," Keieijitsumu, May 1979.

# THE TRANSFER PRICE BASED ON A SHADOW PRICE FOR RESOURCE TRANSFERS AMONG DEPARTMENTS

Yasuhiro Monden

## 1. Introduction

The purpose of this article* is to investigate the usefulness of transfer prices based on a shadow price of an LP model in the decentralized resource transfers among departments.

When resources are transferred among departments, the capacities (resources available) at multiple departments will vary simultaneously as well as costs at the resource-receiving department. If decisions are to be made on resource transfers under such situations by using the shadow-price based transfer price, the stability of this transfer price will be the focus of the problem to be investigated.

The research in applying LP models or shadow prices to transfer prices has appeared in numerous *accounting* articles such as: Dopuch and Drake [1964], Samuels [1965], Bernhard [1968], Manes [1970], Onsi [1970], Godfrey [1971], Abdel-Khalik and Lusk [1974], Onsi [1974], Talwar [1974], Kornbluth [1974], Watson [1975], and Bailey and Boe [1976], etc.

On the other hand, research in sensitivity analysis of LP has also appeared in many *accounting* works such as: Churchill and Steadry [1966], Rappaport [1967], Jensen [1968], Wright [1970], and Hartley [1970], etc.

---

*The author wishes to thank Professor Ronald V. Hartley of Bowling Green State University, Professor James T. Godfrey of the University of Michigan, and Professor Mohamed Onsi of Syracuse University for their guidance and suggestions in writing earlier drafts of this paper.

Taking a step further, in this paper, the author will incorporate both the research of a shadow-price based transfer price and the sensitivity analysis of LP in order to verify the stability of transfer prices under simultaneous changes of multiple parameters. The theoretical research on the dual-price based transfer price and its practical applications should be conducted in the field of accounting rather than in any other institution of learning.

In exploring the theme above, this paper will provide a heuristic approach to resolve the problem of human-resource re-allocation among departments. With this labor turnover, the manpower capacity of each department will be altered, and the labor-receiving departments might have to pay higher wages to the newcomers than to the present employees. In addition, because of their unskilled labor, costs for training might also have to be paid. Under such conditions, we must determine the desirable turnover of human resources from the viewpoint of the company as a whole.

The reason for re-allocation of manpower to become a significant issue is due to the need for effective utilization of fixed wage costs based on the need for permanent employment.[1] For example, there are

---

[1]Traditionally, there is special employment in Japan called *life-time employment* (see Yoshino [1968]). Moreover, there are no *craft unions* in Japan as seen in America and Europe; therefore, *enterprise unions* are prevalent among Japanese firms. Thus, the manpower transfers among departments within a company is conducted more easily in Japan than in America and Europe. Human resource transfers in American and European companies, however, will become necessary because of the tendency to move toward a stabilized form of employment.

Stabilized employment in American companies will tend to move in this direction for two reasons: 1) To employ a new employee from an outside labor market, the firm must pay for training, recruitment, and screening costs. Since these are "quasi fixed costs" of labor, it is better for management to have a continuously stabilized employment relationship rather than create easy layoffs, etc. 2) If an employee is laid off, he must pay to look for a new job or return to his old job. From these two reasons, the conditions for discharges or layoffs by management have been inclined to be constrained. (Doeringer and Piore [1971], p. 74, p. 30).

departments that have sufficient manpower and departments that have insufficient manpower, according to the fluctuations in the market structure. In this paper, we will be investigating the problem of effectively allocating excess manpower of the former departments to the latter.

## 2. Usefulness of Transfer Prices

Assume that the production planning problem of a firm is formulated as follows:

Problem A (in linear programming model form):

$\bar{x}_j$: production of product j

$p_j$: contribution margin of product j (In computing $p_j$, labor costs are subtracted)

$b_i$: labor time available in department i

$a_{ij}$: labor hours to be consumed at department i by one unit of product j.

$$\max: \sum_{j=1}^{n} p_j \bar{x}_j$$

$$\text{s.t.:} \quad \sum_{j=1}^{n} a_{ij} \bar{x}_j \leq b_i \quad (i=1, \ldots, m)$$

$$\bar{x}_j \leq 0. \quad (j=1, \ldots, n)$$

Also denote:

S: optimal basis matrix $[a^*_{ij}]$ in Problem A

P: $(1 \times m)$ vector of $p_j$ corresponding to each column vector in S

$\bar{X}$: $(m \times 1)$ vector of the optimal solution

B: $(m \times 1)$ vector of $b_i$

W: $(1 \times m)$ vector of the shadow price $(W_i)$ for the constraint i, then, the following equations will hold:

$$\bar{X} = S^{-1} B \qquad (1)$$

$$W = P\, S^{-1}. \qquad (2)$$

Now, let's define the transfer price ($t_i$) of one labor time in the manpower-receiving department i as follows:

$$t_i = W_i + c_i, \qquad (3)$$

where we define:

$t_i$: transfer price, i.e., a kind of reward given by the central office in the amount of $t_i$ per labor hour for the receiving department i to absorb excessive manpower from other departments. This is a backward transfer price.[2]

$W_i$: shadow price of one labor hour at the receiving department i. In short, the amount of the contribution margin gained for the company as a whole by each additional input of one labor hour to department i.

$c_i$: wage rate per hour of present labor at the receiving department i.

Since we are considering the problem of transferring manpower among departments, labor costs at each department can be regarded as variable costs which will behave proportionally to the operating level of its department. If there remains some excess labor in the company (even after labor transfers), we can assume that those employees, if not laid off, can be transferred to outside subsidiaries or affiliated companies.[3]

The transfer price $t_i$ is the additional revenue which the receiving department i can gain by an additional input of one labor hour. To obtain this additional revenue, this department i must pay the labor cost of

---

[2]In regards to transfer prices, we can also use the amount of revenue ($T_i$) per week of one additional laborer without using the unit amount per one standard labor hour.

[3]This assumption is made especially for Japanese companies.

$c_i + \alpha_i$ per hour for the transferred laborers from other departments. Therefore, this additional input of labor can pay if the following equation (4) holds:

$$t_i \geq c_i + \alpha_i \tag{4}$$

where $\alpha_i$ is equivalent to the extra incremental amount of the labor cost, which is the difference between the wage rate ($c_i$) of the present labor in department i and the wage rate of transferred manpower. (If $\alpha_i < 0$, the wage rate of the present labor is greater than that of transferring labor). But, $\alpha_i$ includes not only wages, but also training and other turnover costs for the newcomers (transferred employees). Thus, $\alpha_i$ cannot be grasped at the *ex ante* point of time.

Using a profitability test on equation (4), the manager of labor-receiving department i independently makes a decision whether he should accept additional manpower or not. Therefore, it should be noted that here is the *decentralized* decision-making in which the accounting transfer price based on a shadow price will function effectively.

It should be mentioned that, if the wage rate at department i has increased from $c_i$ to $c_i + \alpha_i$ (decreased in the case, $\alpha_i < 0$), the values of shadow prices in the optimal solution will change from the initial $W_i$ to $\bar{W}_i$ because the cost data has changed. In this case, however, the writer proposes the following theorem will always hold:

$$\text{If } W_i \geq \alpha_i, \text{ then} \tag{5}$$

$$\bar{W}_i + (c_i + \alpha_i) = t_i, \tag{6}$$

where $\bar{W}_i$ is the shadow price after the capacities and cost have changed.

Equation (6) can be translated as:

New shadow price + New wage rate = Original transfer price.

In other words, although the value of a shadow price has changed in the new optimal solution under varied conditions, the value of the transferred price ($t_i$) will remain the same. Such stability of the transfer price will hold under situations in which the capacities (labor hours) of multiple departments will fluctuate simultaneously by its labor turnover, and costs at the multiple-receiving departments will also fluctuate simultaneously by the varying amounts of $\alpha_i$.

However, the increase or decrease in the capacities at various departments must be made consistent with each other from the company's viewpoint with a certain methodology (parametric programming for the B vector) which will be described in the next section.

Moreover, the reason for using $t_i$ as a transfer price instead of the shadow price $W_i$ is: 1) the labor cost of a transferred labor hour can be measured directly as $c_i + \alpha_i$ and 2) the value of $t_i$ has the stability described above.

The main purpose of this paper is to propose the above theorem in (5) and (6) and to show mathematical proof for this postulation.

### 3. Production by the Additional Problem

Let's assume in the production planning model of Problem A that there are four departments (i=i, ..., 4), and that in the optimal solution, departments 3 and 4 have excess labor (slack capacities) and departments 1 and 2 are fully operated with no idle capacities. Then, assume again that these idle workers in department 3 can be transferred to the fully-operated departments 1 and 2. By a one-time turnover, two workers can be withdrawn from department 3 and one worker transferred to department 1 and 2, respectively. If the labor hours is 40 hours per week per worker, then the *manpower trading ratio* among departments in this case can be represented as $\beta$ in the following:

$$\beta = \begin{bmatrix} \text{capacity change in department 1} \\ \text{capacity change in department 2} \\ \text{capacity change in department 3} \\ \text{capacity change in department 4} \end{bmatrix} = \begin{bmatrix} 40 \\ 40 \\ -80 \\ 0 \end{bmatrix} ;$$

In general:

$$\beta = \begin{bmatrix} \beta_1 \\ \cdot \\ \cdot \\ \beta_2 \\ \cdot \\ \cdot \\ \beta_i \\ \cdot \\ \cdot \\ \beta_m \end{bmatrix}$$

$\beta$ is the proporation of manpower by a one-time turnover, but, how frequently can we produce this kind of turnover? In this transfer, the optimal basis in the original overall model (Problem A) should not be altered.

In short, the kind of products which were dealt in the optimal solution hitherto, should be consistently produced even after transferring manpower, and should not be exchanged with other new products. We define such number of frequency of manpower turnover in a planning period as $\theta$. Then, the new production plan X after the manpower trading can be calculated by the following equation:

$$X = S^{-1} (B + \theta\beta) \tag{8}$$

where $\theta$ is the frequency of manpower turnover.

Because $X \geq 0$,

$$S^{-1}B + S^{-1}\theta\beta \geq 0, \tag{9}$$

where o is (m × 1) zero vector.[4]

Equation (9) consists of m simultaneous inequalities, and all of which will be satisfied by the following range of $\theta$:

$$\underline{\theta} \leq \theta \leq \bar{\theta} . \tag{10}$$

Because $\theta$ must be nonnegative by definition of $\beta$, equation (10) should be confined to $0 \leq \theta \leq \bar{\theta}$ when $\underline{\theta} \leq 0$ due to (9).

At this stage, in accordance with the receiving department, which has the minimum receiving availability $\theta^*$ (where $\underline{\theta} \leq \theta^* \leq \bar{\theta}$), the central office should make decisions of manpower transfers among all departments in the company in order for it to move to a more improved state of human location.

The following arguments are to prove mathematically the postulation of equation (5) and (6) mentioned above.

Assume that the capacity of $b_i$ of department i was altered by $\theta^*\beta_i$ on account of a manpower turnover, where:

$\beta_i$: the i-th element of a manpower trading ratio $\beta$.

$\theta^*$: the value of the actually receivable $\theta$ by any receiving department within the range of $\theta$ satisfying equation (10).

Let's consider Problem B for producing the same products as Problem A by only using these capacity changes $\theta^*\beta_i$ (i=1, ..., m). (Also note that some of $\beta_i$ have negative values).

---

[4]Refer to Hartley [1976] Chapter 9 for this type of parametric programming. In this paper, we have done a *partial ranging* of $\theta$ without making its *complete ranging*. The reason for this is that if we did make a complete ranging, the receiving department with an originally binding capacity would be unbinding (in its capacity) and the manpower supplying department with an originally unbinding capacity would become binding.

Problem B:

$$\text{max:} \quad \sum_{j=1}^{n} p_j \bar{\bar{x}}_j$$

$$\text{s.t.:} \quad \sum_{j=1}^{n} a_{ij}\bar{\bar{x}}_j \qquad (i=1, \ldots, m)$$

where variable $\bar{\bar{x}}_j$ has no sign constraints. Moreover, assume that Problem B has employed the same basis S as Problem A. In this case, S is the optimal basis for Problem B, which satisfies the simplex criterion, but some variables of its solution may be negative. In other words,

$\bar{\bar{X}}$: the solution vector of Problem B when the basis is S.

$$\bar{\bar{X}} = S^{-1} \cdot \theta^*\beta >, =, \text{ or } < 0. \tag{11}$$

The summation of this $\bar{\bar{X}}$ and the solution $\bar{X}$ of Problem A is equal to X of equation (8):

$$\begin{aligned} X &= \bar{X} + \bar{\bar{X}} \\ &= S^{-1} \ (B + \theta^*\beta) \geq 0. \end{aligned} \tag{12}$$

The dual prices of Problem B, when the basis is S, are determined by the next equation:

$$\text{dual prices} = P\ S^{-1}. \tag{13}$$

The right-hand side of equation (13) is equal to W because of equation (2). Therefore, as long as Problems A and B assume the same S basis, the dual prices of both problems will take the same value W.

Next, provided that the coefficient values in the objective function of Problem B have been altered, what would occur as a result? In other words, the cost has increased by $\alpha_i$ per standard labor hour of each receiving department i.

The significance of $\alpha_i$ has already been described in the explanation of equation (4). The value of $\alpha_i$ in the manpower receiving department is positive, zero, or negative, but, it is always zero in the manpower supplying department.

As described earlier, the labor cost in this model is regarded as a variable cost, in order for Problem B to be transformed into the following:

Problem C:

$$\max: \sum_{j=1}^{n} (p_j - \sum_{i=1}^{m} a_{ij}\alpha_i)\,\overline{\overline{x}}_j$$

$$\text{s.t.}: \sum_{j=1}^{n} a_{ij}\overline{\overline{x}}_j \leq \theta^*\beta_i. \quad : \quad (i=1, \ldots, m)$$

When the costs of Problem B are altered, thus, leading to Problem C, the costs of Problem A are still constant. In other words, the products to be produced by the existing laborers have obviously remained stable in their costs. Hence, the dual price W of Problem A is still constant.

In reference to this, we should summarize the explanations thus far to avoid misunderstanding and confusion:

> *As a production problem, Problem A and Problem C are regarded as different and separated. On the basis of Problem C, however, the optimal basis S of Problem A has been applied, and the* $\theta^*$ *on the right-hand side of the constraint in Problem C has the value within the range of* $[\overline{X} + \overline{\overline{X}} \geq 0]$.

Now, if both Problem B and C have employed the same S basis, then what is the relationship between the dual price $W_i$ of Problem B and the dual price $\overline{W}_i$ of Problem C? In order to examine the relationship, we have provided the *dual* Problems B' and C' corresponding to Problems B and C, respectively.

## 4. Transfer Prices in Problem B' and Problem C'

The dual Problems B' and C' for the respective primal Problems B and C are as follows:

Problem B':

$$\min: \sum_{i=1}^{m} \theta^*\beta_i W_i$$

$$\text{s.t.:} \quad \sum_{i=1}^{m} a_{ij}W_i = p_j \qquad (j=1, \ldots, n)$$

$$W_i \geq 0. \qquad (i=1, \ldots, m)$$

Problem C':

$$\min: \sum_{i=1}^{m} \theta^*\beta_i \overline{W}_i$$

$$\text{s.t.:} \quad \sum_{i=1}^{m} a_{ij}\overline{W}_i = p_j - \sum_{i=1}^{m} a_{ij}\alpha_i \qquad (j=1, \ldots, n)$$

$$\overline{W}_i \geq 0. \qquad (i=1, \ldots, m)$$

The reason why both constraints of Problems B' and C' are only equality types is due to the non-existence of sign constraints on variable $\overline{\overline{x}}_j$ in Problems B and C.

In regard to this point, we will set the following in respect to Problem B':

$$W_i - \alpha_i = W_i^*, \tag{14}$$

where we assume:

$$W_i^* \geq 0, \quad \text{or,}$$

$$W_i \geq \alpha_i. \tag{15}$$

It will be described later that this assumption will always be satisifed. Then, by substituting $(W_i^* + \alpha_i)$ for $W_i$, Problem B' can be formulated as the following:

Problem B":

$$\min: \sum_{i=1}^{m} \theta^*\beta_i W_i^* + \sum_{i=1}^{m} \theta^*\beta_i\alpha_i$$

$$\text{s.t.}: \sum_{i=1}^{m} a_{ij}W_i^* = p_j - \sum_{i=1}^{m} a_{ij}\alpha_i \qquad (j=1, \ldots, n)$$

$$W_i^* \geq 0. \qquad (i=1, \ldots, m)$$

The second item $\sum_{i=1}^{m} \theta^*\beta_i\alpha_i$ in the objective function of Problem B" is regarded as a constant value and can be neglected from the viewpoint of introducing the optimal solution. Thus, Problem B" and C are equivalent to each other. Therefore,

$$W_i^* = \overline{W}_i. \qquad (16)$$

Since $W_i^* = W_i - \alpha_i$ according to equation (14), equation (16) then becomes:

$$W_i - \alpha_i = \overline{W}_i. \qquad (17)$$

$$\therefore \quad W_i = \overline{W}_i + \alpha_i. \qquad (18)$$

Adding $c_i$ to both sides of equation (18) we obtain the equation:

$$W_i + c_i = \overline{W}_i + (c_i + \alpha_i). \qquad (19)$$

The left-hand side of equation (19) has been defined as the transfer price $t_i$ of equation (3). Hence, equation (19) becomes:

$$t_i = \overline{W}_i + (c_i + \alpha_i). \qquad (20)$$

Equation (20) is the postulated equation (6) for the stability of a transfer price.

Thus, it was proved that equation (20) should always hold within the range of equation (20). In other words, the original transfer price $t_i$ will always hold as long as $\alpha_i$ does not exceed the original shadow price $W_i$.

Next, if the value of $\alpha_{i*}$ in a specified receiving department i* has increased to the value of $W_{i*}$, then from equation (17) we obtain the following:

$$\overline{W}_i = W_{i*} - \alpha_{i*} = 0.$$

At this time, the *complementary slackness theorem* of LP will make the capacity of this receiving department i* unbinding, and thus, the labor of this department will become excessive. (In other words, the slack variable of the capacity of department i* will join the group of basis variables, though the case will be different if there is a tie profitability with some original basis variable among non-basis variables). Therefore, regarding department i, where $W_i \leq \alpha_i$ on accounting of the large value in $\alpha_i$, no labor should be transferred.

This rule is guaranteed by the decentralized decisions using a transfer price, in which equation (4) always holds. With the decentralized decisions, we have the following:

$$t_i \geq c_i + \alpha_i \qquad (4)$$

could be guaranteed. Substituting equation (3) for $t_i$ we obtain the following:

$$W_i + c_i \geq c_i + \alpha_i.$$

As a result, the assumption equation (15),

$$W_i \geq \alpha_i$$

will always be satisfied.

Moreover, the postulation consisting of equations (15) and (20) will hold only in the fully-operated department i (i.e., non-idle department i), and, in addition, hold in any fully-operated department independently with any cost level in other fully-operated departments i' as well.

In other words, although the changes in $\alpha_i$ value may accrue within the range of equation (20) of each receiving department i *independently with each other*, equation (18) will always hold for each department i.

Further, the theorem equations (15) and (20) will not only hold in the case where $\alpha_i$ has accrued merely in Problem B, but, in addition, where $\alpha_i$ has accrued simultaneously in Problems B and A.

For example, after additional manpower is received by department i, the manager might increase the wage rates of all labor in this department uniformly up to $(c_i + \alpha_i)$. If this occurs, the theorem equations (15) and (20) will still hold. This can be proven easily using a similar verifying process as described above.

## 5. Conclusion

In this paper, we have investigated a heuristic method to re-allocate human resources among departments by using a transfer price based on a shadow price. Thus, we can summarize its solution procedure in the form of a flow chart as shown in Figure 1. With this procedure, it is certain that we can go to some improved state of manpower location if not an optimal state.

Lastly, let's examine why a heuristic solving method is useful for the manpower transferring problem. When we consider the problem of manpower allocations, we must take into account the various degrees of labor specialization in each department under the present allocated status quo. Each department employee has his own specialized level of skill, based on the present technological equipment, product mix, production quantities, etc. In other words, each department needs its own skilled labor. But, the newcomers to other departments are usually unskilled for the job; therefore; "training costs" are needed to polish their skill.

Figure 1. Heuristic Program for Manpower Transfers

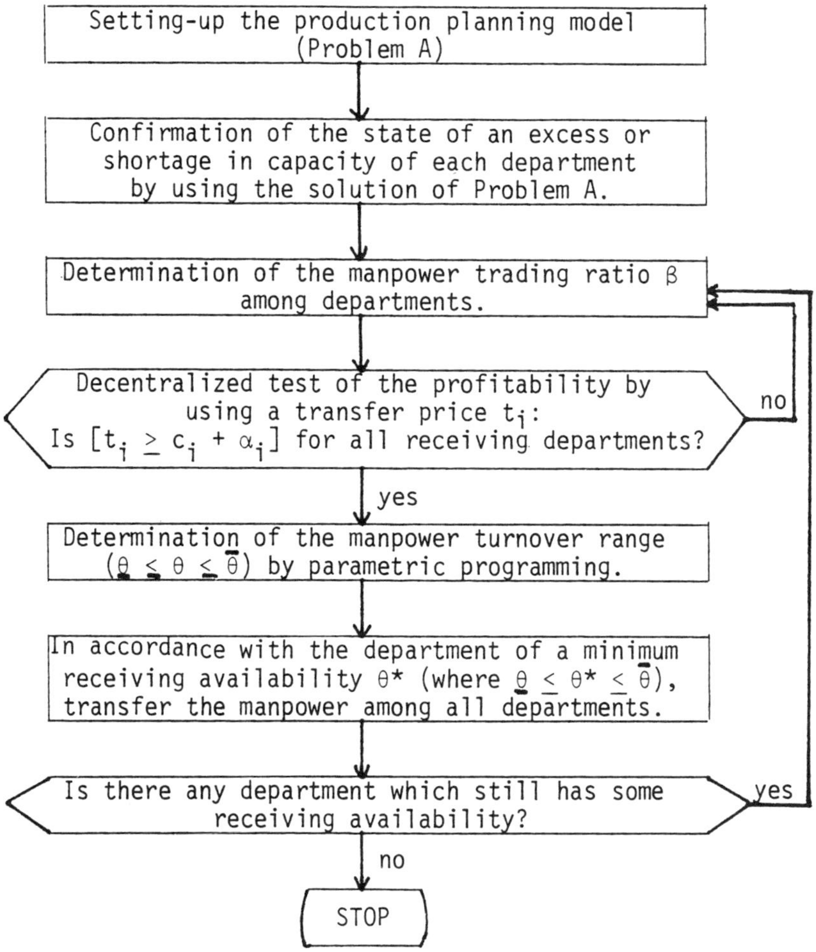


Thus, because of present labor specialization in each department, it becomes impossible to make unconstrained turnovers of human resources among departments, as well as having a wide range of turnovers.

Furthermore, since additional costs $(\alpha_i)$ such as training costs, etc. accompanying transfers are unknown at the central office in an *ex ante* point of time, it is desirable to have a system where each department takes costs into account, and makes decentralized judgments whether or not it is profitable to accept the additional manpower. This system is especially good for the company that has a decentralized profitability for its divisions.

## REFERENCES

1. Abdel-Khalik, A. R. and Lusk, E. J., "Transfer Pricing - A Synthesis," The Accounting Review (January, 1974), pp. 8-23.

2. Baily, A. D. and Boe, W. J., "Goal and Resource Transfers in the Multiple Organization," The Accounting Review (July, 1976), pp. 559-73.

3. Bernhard, R. H., "Some Problems in Applying Mathematical Programming to Opportunity Costing," Journal of Accounting Research (Spring, 1968), pp. 143-48.

4. Churchill, N. C. and Stedry, A. C., "Some Developments in Management Science and Information Systems with Respect to Measurement in Accounting," Jaedicke, R. K., Ijiri, Y., and Nielsen, O., (eds.) Research in Accounting Measurement (American Accounting Association, 1966).

5. Demski, J. S., "Some Consideration in Sensitizing an Optimization Model," The Journal of Industrial Engineering (September, 1968), pp. 463-67.

6. Doeringer, P. B. and Piore, M. J., Internal Labor Market and Manpower Analysis (D. C. Heath and Company, 1971).

7. Dopuch, N. and Drake, D. F., "Accounting Implications of Mathematical Programming Approach to the Transfer Pricing Problem," Journal of Accounting Research (Spring, 1964), pp. 10-24.

8. Godfrey, J. T., "Short-Run Planning in a Decentralized Firm," The Accounting Review (April, 1971), pp. 286-97.

9. Hartley, R. V., "Some Extensions of Sensitivity Analysis," The Accounting Review (April, 1970), pp. 223-34.

10. Hartley, R.V., Operations Research: A Managerial Emphasis, (Goodyear, 1976).

11. Jensen, R. E., "Sensitivity Analysis and Integer Linear Programming," The Accounting Review (July, 1968), pp. 425-46.

12. Kornbluth, J. S., "Accounting in Multiple Objective Linear Programming," The Accounting Review (April, 1974), pp. 284-95.

13. Manes, R. P., "Birch Paper Company Revised: An Exercise in Transfer Pricing," The Accounting Review (January, 1974), pp. 129-31.

14. Onsi, M., "A Transfer Pricing System Based on Opportunity Costs," The Accounting Review (July, 1970), pp. 535-43.

15. Onsi, M., "Transfer Pricing System Based on Opportunity Costs: A Reply," The Accounting Review (January, 1974), pp. 129-31.

16. Rappaport, A., "Sensitivity Analysis in Decision Making," The Accounting Review (July, 1967), pp. 441-56.

17. Rueflie, T. W., "A Generalized Goal Decomposition Model," Management Science (April, 1971), pp. B-649-57.

18. Rueflie, T. W., "Behavioral Externalities in Decentralized Organizations," Management Science (June, 1971), pp. B649-B-657.

19. Samuels, J. M., "Opportunity Costing: An Application of Mathematical Programming," Journal of Accounting Research (Autumn, 1965), pp. 182-91.

20. Talwar, A. K., "Transfer Pricing System Based on Opportunity Costs: A Comment," The Accounting Review (January, 1974), pp. 126-28.

21. Watson, J. H. and Baumler, J. V., "Transfer Pricing: A Behavioral Context," The Accounting Review (July, 1965), pp. 466-74.

22. Wright, F. K., "Dual Variables in Inventory Measurement," The Accounting Review (January, 1970), pp. 129-33.

23. Yoshino, M. Y., Japan's Managerial System: Tradition and Innovation (The MIT Press, 1968).

# A REEXAMINATION OF NET PRESENT VALUE MODEL

By Kiyoshi Okamoto and Setsuo Ohnari

## Introduction

The net present value model used in capital budgeting has been refined in connection with the treatment of risk attitudes under uncertainty. Although such refinement should be encouraged, much improvement in making rational investment decisions and their control might be made by reexamining the underlying assumptions of the decision model itself under certainty. In the traditional model,

$$NPV = \sum_{i=1}^{n} P_i \quad (1 + r)^{-i} - \text{Outlay}$$

one of the underlying assumptions is that the money will earn a certain percentage of interest compounded annually; in other words, the interst is compounded once at the end of each year. In certain cases this does not hold. A fixed deposit in a local post office can earn interest compounded semi-annually. Hence, if we increase the number of times of compounding in a year, we may have models that are continually compounding or discounting. But, we cannot adopt them, because the "compounding annually assumption" is more appropriate for our business practice. A business firm may borrow a certain amount of investment fund. Its interest is usually compounded not instantaneously but annually.

The other underlying assumption is that cash outflows and inflows in an investment take place in a lump sum amount at the end (or at the beginning) of the year. However, this assumption is unrealistic. In practice, cash flows take place monthly, daily, and even instantaneously. The bias in using year-end-cash-flow formulas may not be negligible for investment decisions. Moreover, this assumption is inappropriate for controlling capital expenditures on a monthly basis. Business management using the traditional model cannot compare actual costs with budgeted costs until the end of the year.

Based on these reasons we will improve the net present value model by eliminating the second assumption, while still holding the first.

## Cash Inflows with Monthly Fluctuations

Now, let's concentrate on cash inflows in an investment. The business man in Japan often speaks of "2-8", literally, February and August, which are the two slackest months in the year. Thus, we will take cash inflows with seasonal fluctuations into consideration in our model.

According to commercial practice in Japan, most cash inflows take place at the end of each month, while, in some businesses they take place instantaneously. Therefore, we will construct two models: a discrete model, and a continuous one.

## Monthly Cash Outflows for Building an Investment

When an investment is for purchasing a machine or some other fixed assets, then we can safely assume that the cash outflows will take place in a lump sum at the beginning of the year. But, if an investment is for building a large-size machine or plant, we should assume that cash outflows will take place at the end of each month for several periods. Here, we will consider the latter case.

Interest for a Fractional Period Shorter Than a Year

As the two models take into consideration monthly fluctuations in cash flows, we must determine how to treat the interest for a fractional period less than a year.

There are two alternative methods. One is to calculate the interest on a compound interest basis:

$$FV = PV\ (1 + r)^{\frac{j}{12}}$$

where

FV = future value of the principal

PV = present value of the principal

r = annual percentage rate of interest

j = number of months

The other is to calculate the interest on the simple interest basis:

$$FV = PV\ (1 + \tfrac{j}{12}r).$$

We will adopt the latter method in accordance with our commercial practice.

A Discrete Model with Monthly Fluctuating Cash Flows

Let us calculate the net present value of an investment. The origin of the time axis which is coordinated by t denotes the time of the beginning of operation. For $k = 1, 2, \ldots\ldots, m$ and $j = 1, 2, \ldots\ldots, 12$, $t = -k + 1 - \frac{j}{12}$ denotes the time of k - 1 years and j months before the operation begins and for $i = 1, 2, \ldots\ldots, n$ and $j = 1, 2, \ldots\ldots, 12$, $t = i - 1 + \frac{j}{12}$ denotes i - 1 years and j months after the operation begins.

We assume that for $k = 1, 2, \ldots\ldots, m$ and $j = 1, 2, \ldots\ldots, 12$, cash outflows $I_j^{(k)}$ for the construction periods will take place discretely at time $t = -k + 1 - \frac{j}{12}$ and for $i = 1, 2, \ldots\ldots, n$ and $j = 1, 2, \ldots\ldots, 12$,

cash inflows $P_j^{(i)}$ will take place discretely at time $t = i - 1 + \frac{j}{12}$.
Then, we clearly obtain the following formula:

$$NPV = \sum_{i=1}^{n} \sum_{j=1}^{12} P_j^{(i)} (1 + r)^{-i+1} \quad (1 + \frac{j}{12}r)$$

$$- \sum_{k=1}^{m} \sum_{j=1}^{12} I_j^{(k)} (1 + r)^{k-1} (1 + \frac{j}{12}r)$$

Continuous Model

We assume that cash inflows will take place continuously over the time interval [0, n], while cash outflows will take place discretely.

Now, we will introduce the cash inflow density function $f_i$, $i = 1, 2, \ldots\ldots, n$, $f_i$ is a real valued piecewise continuous function defined on closed time interval [i-1, i]. And, for two arbitrary times $t_1$ and $t_2$, $i-1 \leqq t_1 < t_2 \leqq i$, the total sum of cash inflows taking place in the interval $[t_1, t_2]$ is calculated by

$$\int_{t_1}^{t_2} f_i(t)dt.$$

Let's divide the time interval [i-1, i] into $\ell_i$ subintervals; namely

$$i-1 = t_0^{(i)} < t_1^{(i)} < t_2^{(i)} < \ldots\ldots < t_{\ell_i-1}^{(i)} < t_{\ell_i}^{(i)} = i$$

and $\xi_j^{(i)}$ is defined by

$$\int_{t_{j-1}^{(i)}}^{t_j^{(i)}} f_i(t)dt = f_i\ (\xi_j^{(i)})\ (t_j^{(i)} - t_{j-1}^{(i)}),\ t_{j-1}^{(i)} \leqq \xi_j^{(i)} \leqq t_j^{(i)},\ j = 1,$$

$2, \cdots, \ell_i$.

Let us assume also that the total sum of cash inflows in the interval $[t_{j-1}^{(i)}, t_j^{(i)}]$ take place at time $\xi_j^{(i)}$. Then we can calculate the value at time t = i-1 as follows:

$$\sum_{j=1}^{\ell_i} f_i\,(\xi_j^{(i)})\,(t_j^{(i)} - t_{j-1}^{(i)})\,\{1 + r(\xi_j^{(i)} - (i - 1))\}^{-1}$$

Then let $k_i \longrightarrow +\infty$ and $t_j^{(i)} - t_{j-1}^{(i)} \longrightarrow 0$ for all j = 1, 2, ....., $\ell_i$.

It clearly converges to:

$$\int_{i-1}^{i} f_i(t)\,\{1 + r(t - (i - 1))\}^{-1}dt.$$

Accordingly, we obtain the following formula:

$$NPV = \sum_{i=1}^{n} (1 + r)^{-i+1} \int_{i-1}^{i} f_i(t)\,\{1+r\,(t - i + 1)\}^{-1}dt$$

$$- \sum_{k=1}^{m} \sum_{j=1}^{12} I_j^{(k)}\,(1 + r)^{-k+1}\,(1 + \tfrac{j}{12}r)$$

## An Illustration for the Discrete Model

To illustrate the nature of our discrete model, suppose a firm is reviewing a project that involves cash outflows of $50,000 for a new equipment which is determined to have a useful life of three years. It will take three months to construct the equipment and cash outflows for the construction will take place in the following way,

Exhibit 1

Cash Outflows for the Construction

| | | |
|---|---|---|
| Three months prior | | $20,000 |
| Two months prior | | 10,000 |
| One month prior | | 10,000 |
| Time of completion | | 10,000 |
| | Total | $50,000 |

The firm estimates that, with this equipment, an output of 20,000 units per year can be produced and distributed at variable costs of $2.00 per unit plus fixed cash expenditures of $32,400 per year with the unit sales price at $5.00.

It also estimates the seasonal monthly fluctuation rates of sales volume in units, shown below in Exhibit 2.

Exhibit 2

Monthly Fluctuation of Sales Volume

| Month | Rate (%) | Volume in Units |
|---|---|---|
| January | 9.0 | 1,800 |
| February | 6.4 | 1,280 |
| March | 7.0 | 1,400 |
| April | 8.5 | 1,700 |
| May | 9.6 | 1,920 |
| June | 10.0 | 2,000 |
| July | 8.0 | 1,600 |
| August | 5.0 | 1,000 |
| September | 6.0 | 1,200 |
| October | 8.4 | 1,680 |
| November | 10.6 | 2,120 |
| December | 11.5 | 2,300 |
| Total | 100.0 | 20,000 |

It depreciates equipment on a straight-line basis. The salvage proceeds of $5,000 are expected at the end of the third year. The net income generated by the equipment will be taxed at a rate of 40% and the tax will be paid in the next February. For illustrative purposes, we assume that the firm's management believes a 10% discount rate is appropriate for discounting the after-tax cash flows for this type of investment project. The construction of the equipment will be completed at the end of December and operation begins at the beginning of January in the first year.

(1) Net present value with the traditional model

With the conditions described above, the net present value of the project is computed by the traditional model as follows:

Exhibit 3

Net Present Value by the Traditional Model

| Year | | 0 | 1 | 2 | 3 |
|---|---|---|---|---|---|
| Outlay | | (\$50,000) | | | |
| Net cash flows after tax from operations | | | | | |
| (1-0.4)27,600[(a)] + 15,000[(b)] x 0.4 | | | \$22,560 | \$22,560 | \$22,560 |
| Salvage at end of 3 years | | | | | 5,000 |
| Present value of cash inflows | | | | | |
| 2.4869 x 22,560 | 56,104 | | | | |
| 0.7513 x 5,000 | 3,757 | | | | |
| totals | \$59,861 | | | | |
| Net present value | \$ 9,861 | | | | |

(a) net cash inflows from operations in each period: (\$5.00 - \$2.00) x 20,000 - \$32,400 = \$27,600

(b) annual depreciation: (\$50,000 - \$5,000) ÷ 3 = \$15,000

(2) Net present value with the discrete model

1) Present value of investment outlay

Because our discrete model acknowledged monthly cash flows, the present value of investment outlay during the construction period is computed as follows:

Exhibit 4

Present Value of Investment Outlay

| | |
|---|---|
| $\$20{,}000\ (1 + \frac{3}{12} \times \frac{1}{10})$ ............... | $20,500 |
| $\$10{,}000\ (1 + \frac{2}{12} \times \frac{1}{10})$ ............... | $10,167 |
| $\$10{,}000\ (1 + \frac{1}{12} \times \frac{1}{10})$ ............... | $10,083 |
| $10,000 | $10,000 |
| Total | $50,750 |

2) Monthly net cash inflows from opeartions

Equipment operation begins at the beginning of January in the first year. Thus, monthly net cash inflows from operations for the first six months, for example, are shown in Exhibit 5.

Exhibit 5

Budgeted Monthly Net Cash Inflows From Operations

| Month | Sales Volume in Units | Contribution Margin @ $3.00(= $5.00 - $2.00) | Fixed Cash Expenditures | Net Cash Inflow |
|---|---|---|---|---|
| January | 1,800 | $ 5,400 | $ 2,700 | $ 2,700 |
| February | 1,280 | 3,840 | 2,700 | 1,140 |
| March | 1,400 | 4,200 | 2,700 | 1,500 |
| April | 1,700 | 5,100 | 2,700 | 2,400 |
| May | 1,920 | 5,760 | 2,700 | 3,060 |
| June | 2,000 | 6,000 | 2,700 | 3,300 |
| . | . | . | . | . |
| . | . | . | . | . |
| . | . | . | . | . |
| December | 2,300 | 6,900 | 2,700 | 4,200 |
| | $20,000 | $60,000 | $32,400 | $27,600 |

3) Net present value computation

Exhibit 6 shows the net present value computation. We can find that the total investment outlay is to be recovered by the end of June in the third year and net present value of the project is $12,072, which is $2,211 more than the result using the traditional model.

Exhibit 6

Net Present Value Computation

| Month | Present Value of Cash Inflow | Cumulative Present Value of Cash Inflows | Unrecovered Investment at end of month |
|---|---|---|---|
| (The 1st year) | | | $(50,750) |
| January | $2,678 (c) | $2,678 | (48,072) |
| February | 1,121 | 3,799 | (46,951) |
| March | 1,463 | 5,262 | (45,488) |
| April | 2,323 | 7,585 | (43,165) |
| May | 2,938 | 10,523 | (40,227) |
| June | 3,143 | 13,666 | (37,084) |
| . | . | . | . |
| . | . (omitted) | . | . |
| . | . | . | . |
| (The 3rd year) | | | |
| . | . | . | . |
| . | . | . | . |
| May | 2,428 | 49,918 | (832) |
| June | 2,597 | 52,515 | 1,765 |
| July | 1,640 | 54,155 | 3,405 |
| August | 232 | 54,387 | 3,637 |
| September | 692 | 55,079 | 4,329 |
| October | 1,785 | 56,864 | 6,114 |
| November | 2,771 | 59,635 | 8,885 |
| December | 6,912 | 66,547 | 15,797 |
| (The 4th year) | | | |
| February | (3,725) (d) | 62,822 | 12,072 |

(c) $\$2,700 \div (1 + \frac{1}{12} \times \frac{1}{10}) = \$2,678$

(d) tax for the 3rd year: ($27,600 - $15,000) x 0.4 = $5,040
$\$5,040 \div (1 + \frac{1}{10})^3\ (1 + \frac{2}{12} \times \frac{1}{10}) = \$3,725$

(3) Post audit in our discrete model

Assume that six months have passed since the equipment was placed in operation and the following actual data was obtained:

1) Actual outlay for the construction

| | |
|---|---|
| Three months before | $20,200 |
| Two months before | 10,100 |
| One month before | 10,100 |
| At the time of completion | 10,100 |
| Total | $50,500 |

2) Actual net cash inflows

Exhibit 7

Actual Monthly Net Cash Flows from Operations

| Month | Sales Volume in Units | Contribution Margin @ $2.95 (=$5.05 - $2.10) | Fixed Cash Expenditures | Net Cash Inflows |
|---|---|---|---|---|
| January | 1,650 | $4,867.5 | $2,750 | $2,117.5 |
| February | 1,100 | 3,245.0 | 2,750 | 495.0 |
| March | 1,240 | 3,658.0 | 2,750 | 908.0 |
| April | 1,500 | 4,425.0 | 2,750 | 1,675.0 |
| May | 1,778 | 5,245.1 | 2,750 | 2,495.1 |
| June | 1,822 | 5,374.9 | 2,750 | 2,624.9 |
| Total | $9,090 | $26,815.5 | $16,500 | $10,315.5 |

Then we can ascertain whether the project has realized the anticipated benefits so far. For the purpose of the post audit, actual cash flows are compared with budgeted cash flows on the present value basis and variances are analyzed in the following way:

I. Construction variance

Present value of budgeted investment outlay . . . . . $50,750

Less: Present value of actual investment outlay

| | | |
|---|---|---|
| $\$20,200\ (1 + \frac{3}{12} \times \frac{1}{10})$ . . | $20,705 | |
| $10,100\ (1 + \frac{2}{12} \times \frac{1}{10})$ . . | 10,268 | |
| $10,100\ (1 + \frac{1}{12} \times \frac{1}{10})$ . . | 10,184 | |
| $10,100 \times 1$ . . . . . . . . | 10,100 | |
| | 51,257 | 51,257 |
| Construction variance . . . . . . . . | | ($ 507) (U) |

U = Unfavorable

II. Cash inflows variance

(1) Total variance

Cumulative present value of budgeted cash inflows for the first six months . . . . . $13,666

Cumulative present value of actual cash inflow for the same periods

$\frac{\$2,117.5}{1 + \frac{1}{12} \times \frac{1}{10}}$ . . . . . . . . . 2,100

$\frac{495.0}{1 + \frac{2}{12} \times \frac{1}{10}}$ . . . . . . . . . 487

$\frac{908.0}{1 + \frac{3}{12} \times \frac{1}{10}}$ . . . . . . . . . 886

$\frac{1,675.0}{1 + \frac{4}{12} \times \frac{1}{10}}$ . . . . . . . . . 1,621

$\frac{2,495.1}{1 + \frac{5}{12} \times \frac{1}{10}}$ . . . . . . . . . 2,395

| | | |
|---|---|---|
| $\frac{2,624.9}{1 + \frac{6}{12} \times \frac{1}{10}}$ . . . . . . . . . | 2,500 | |
| Total . . . . . . | \$ 9,989 | \$ 9,989 |
| Total Variance | | \$ 3,677 |

(2) Analysis of total variance

The total variance can be analyzed into sales price variance, sales quantity variance, variable cost variance and fixed cash expenditure variance.

Let CI = net cash inflows

P = unit sales price

X = sales volume in units

v = unit variable costs

F = fixed cash expenditures

b subscript = budgeted amount

a subscript = actual amount

Then

$$CI_a - CI_b = \underbrace{(P_a - P_b)\, X_a}_{\text{sales price variance}} + \underbrace{(X_a - X_b)\,(P_b - V_b)}_{\text{sales quantity variance}} + \underbrace{(V_b - V_a)\, X_a}_{\text{variable cost variance}} + \underbrace{(F_b - F_a)}_{\text{fixed cash expenditure variance}}$$

Of course, these variances should be discounted to the present value. Now, in our case, each variance in the first January can be computed as follows:

a. sales price variance

$$\frac{(\$505 - \$500) \times 1,650}{1 + \frac{1}{12} \times \frac{1}{10}} = \$8,182$$

b. sales quantity variance

$$\frac{(1{,}650 - 1{,}800)\ \$3.00}{1 + \frac{1}{12} \times \frac{1}{10}} = -\$446.28$$

c. variable cost variance

$$\frac{(\$2.00 - \$2.10) \times 1{,}650}{1 + \frac{1}{12} \times \frac{1}{10}} = -\ \$1{,}636$$

d. fixed cash expenditure variance

$$\frac{\$2{,}700 - \$2{,}750}{1 + \frac{1}{12} \times \frac{1}{10}} = \$496$$

In the same way the total present value of each variance for the first six months can be computed. Only the computation results are shown.

| | | |
|---|---|---|
| sales price variance | $ 441 | (F) |
| sales quantity variance | ($2,944) | (U) |
| variable cost variance | ($ 882) | (U) |
| fixed cash expenditure variance | ($ 292) | (U) |
| total variance | ($3,677) | (U) |

F = Favorable U = Unfavorable

## III. Margin of investment safety

Lastly, we can evaluate the impact of all variances on the investment decision. A simple, but practical rough index for the margin of investment safety may be the comparison of variances with the budgeted net present value:

$$\frac{\$12{,}072 - (\$507 + \$3{,}677)}{\$12{,}072} = 65.3\%$$

Thus, we know that about 34.7% of investment safety has been lost for the first six months.

## Conclusion

The basic two assumptions in the traditional net present value model have been mentioned in cost accounting literature, but they were often mingled together. We believe that both assumptions should be distinguished from each other.

The "compounding annually assumption" is appropriate for our business practice, while the "year-end-cash-flow assumption" is entirely unrealistic. Holding still the first assumption, we should adopt the "month-end-or instantaneous-cash-flow assumption" in the net present value model. Whether the bias in using traditional year-end-cash-flow formulas is considered negligible or not is dependent on the size of the investment and on the cost of capital.

Even if it is considered negligible, the traditional model is inappropriate for post audits of capital expenditures. Unfortunately, these audits have seldom been very successful. There might be many reasons. One reason may be the difficulty to isolate the portion of the company's profit stemming from a specific investment. The other may be the conflict of DCF models and the accrual-accounting models. It is no doubt, however, that the adoption of monthly or continuous cash flows in the net present value model is an essential step toward the integration of decision and control models.

# DECISION PROCEDURES IN TWO LEVEL HIERARCHICAL ORGANIZATIONS

by Koichi Miyasawa

## 1. Formulation of the Problem

We consider an organization consisting of the superior decision unit $D_0$ and n inferior decision units $D_i$, i=1,...,n. They face the state of the nature x which is an element of the state space X. It is assumed that each decision unit $D_i$ has its own prior probability law $\phi_i$ on X, i=0,1,...,n. The task of the superior decision unit $D_0$ is to give a command $\gamma$ in the given set $\Gamma$ to each inferior decision unit $D_i$, i=1,...,n.

Case I We shall consider first the case where a command $\gamma\varepsilon\Gamma$ specifies to each $D_i$, i=1,...,n: 1) the action space $A_i$ from which $D_i$ must choose an action $a_i$—this may correspond to the allocation of resources from $D_0$ to $D_i$.; 2) the objective function $\omega_i(\cdot|\gamma)$ which is the function of the action $a_i$ chosen by $D_i$ itself, and the actions $a_j$ chosen by $D_i$ itself, and the actions $a_j$ chosen by other inferior decision units $D_j$, $j\neq i$, and the true state of the nature x, i.e.,

$$\omega_i\equiv\omega_i(a;x|\gamma),\ \text{where}\ a=(a_1,---,a_n), \tag{1.1}$$

and 3) the information structure $\eta_i$, which is the function from X to a certain space $Y_i$, i.e., when $x\varepsilon X$ is the true state of the nature, $D_i$ observes the value $y_i=\eta_i(x)$.

The task of each inferior decision unit $D_i$ after receiving a command $\gamma$ from $D_0$ is to choose a decision rule $\alpha_i$ which is based on his given information structure $\eta_i$, i.e., a function $\alpha_i$ from $Y_i$ to $A_i$, i=1,...,n.

If the decision units $D_i$, $i=1,\ldots,n$ choose the decision rules $\alpha_i,\ldots,\alpha_n$, then the expected payoff to $D_i$ is given by

$$\Omega_i(\alpha|\gamma)=E_{\phi_i}\{\omega_i(\alpha([\eta(x)]);x|\gamma)\}, \tag{1.2}$$

where

$$\alpha=(\alpha_1,\ldots,\alpha_n),\ \alpha[\eta(x)]=(\alpha_1(\eta_1(x)),\ldots,\alpha_n(\eta_n(x))). \tag{1.3}$$

Here we shall assume the given overall payoff function $\omega$ to the organization itself is given by a certain function $\psi(\cdot)$ of $\omega_1,\ldots,\omega_n$, i.e.,

$$\omega(a_1,\ldots,a_n;x)=\psi(\omega_1(a;x),\ldots,\omega_n(a;x)). \tag{1.4}$$

Generally speaking, it may be a rather difficult problem to define properly the function $\psi$. On the other hand it may occur in the cases where $\omega$ is naturally given by

$$\omega=\omega_1+\ldots+\omega_n. \tag{1.5}$$

Now it is assumed that under a given command $\gamma$, each inferior decision unit $D_i$ is motivated to choose a decision rule $\alpha_i$ which gives a higher expected payoff $\Omega_i$ to him under the given command $\gamma$. But $\Omega_i$ depends not only on $D_i$'s decision rule $\alpha_i$ but also on the decision rules $\alpha_j$, chosen by other inferior decision units $D_j$, $j\neq i$. Thus, we define

Definition 1. A decision rule $\hat{\alpha}(\gamma)=(\hat{\alpha}_1(\gamma),\ldots,\hat{\alpha}_n(\gamma))$ is called Nash-equilibrium (N.e.) under a command $\gamma$, if the following condition holds: for each i, $i=1,\ldots,n$,

$$\Omega_i(\alpha_i,\hat{\alpha}(\gamma)|\gamma)\leq\Omega_i(\hat{\alpha}(\gamma)\ |\gamma), \tag{1.6}$$

for all $\alpha_i$, where $\Omega_i(\alpha,\hat{\alpha})\equiv\Omega_i(\hat{\alpha}_1,\ldots,\alpha_i,\ldots,\hat{\alpha}_n)$.

It is clear that if $\omega_1=\ldots=\omega_n=\omega$ and $\phi_1=\ldots=\phi_n=\phi_o$, then the inferior decision units $D_1,\ldots,D_n$ may be considered as forming a team and then a N.e. decision rule is one that is person by person satisfactory (p.b.p.s.) in Marschak's sense [1].

Concerning the behavior of the inferior decision units we assume

Behavioral Assumption 1. Each inferior decision unit $D_i$, $i=1,\ldots,n$, receiving a command $\gamma$ from $D_0$ is satisfied by choosing a N.e. decision rule $\hat{\alpha}(\gamma)=(\hat{\alpha}_1(\gamma),\ldots,\hat{\alpha}_n(\gamma))$ and by attaining the expected payoff

$$\hat{\Omega}_i(\gamma)\equiv\Omega_i(\hat{\alpha}(\gamma)|\gamma), \quad i=1,\ldots,n. \tag{1.7}$$

Now let $\Gamma^0$ be the set of all commands $\gamma\varepsilon\Gamma$ for which a N.e. decision rule $\hat{\alpha}(\gamma)$ exists. If $D_0$ orders a command $\gamma\varepsilon\Gamma^0$ to $D_i$, $i=1,\ldots,n$, then by Behavioral Assumption 1, they will choose a N.e. decision rule $\hat{\alpha}(\gamma)$ corresponding to $\gamma$, and the overall expected payoff is given by

$$\hat{\Omega}(\gamma)=E_{\phi_0}\{\psi(\hat{\omega}_1(\gamma),\ldots,\hat{\omega}_n(\gamma))\}, \tag{1.8}$$

where

$$\hat{\omega}_i(\gamma)=\omega_i(\hat{\alpha}(\gamma)[\eta(x)];x|\gamma),\ i=1,\ldots,n\ . \tag{1.9}$$

In the special case of (1.5), if $\phi_0=\phi_1=\ldots=\phi_n$, then we have

$$\hat{\Omega}(\gamma)=\hat{\Omega}_1(\gamma)+\ldots+\hat{\Omega}_n(\gamma)\ . \tag{1.10}$$

Behavioral Assumption 2. The organization itself is satisfied by the superior decision $D_0$ ordering the command $\gamma^0\varepsilon\Gamma^0$, such that

$$\max_{\gamma\varepsilon\Gamma^0}\hat{\Omega}(\gamma)=\hat{\Omega}(\gamma^0)\ , \tag{1.11}$$

and we shall call such $\gamma^0$ an optimal command by $D_0$.

Thus, in our two-level hierarchical organization, the inferior decision units $D_i$, $i=1,\ldots,n$ and the organization itself are all satisfied when $D_0$ orders an optimal command $\gamma^0$, and then $D_i$, $i=1,\ldots,n$ choose the corresponding N.e. decision rule $\hat{\alpha}(\gamma^0)$. Our task, then, is to find $\gamma^0$ and $\hat{\alpha}(\gamma^0)$.

Case II In contrast to the above approach, the case may occur where the overall payoff function $\omega$ to the organization is given beforehand as the function of the actions $a_1\varepsilon A_i$ chosen by the inferior decision units $D_i$, $i=1,\ldots,n$ and the true states of the nature $x\varepsilon X$, i.e.,

$$\omega=\omega(a_1\ldots,a_n;x) \ . \tag{1.12}$$

In this case, we assume that a command $\gamma$ by $D_0$ consists of two components $\zeta$ and $\eta$, i.e.,

$$\gamma=(\zeta,\eta) \ , \tag{1.13}$$

where: 1) $\zeta$ assigns the objective function $\omega_i$ to the inferior decision unit $D_i$, $i=1,\ldots,n$, which is a function of $a=(a_1,\ldots,a_n)$ and $x$, such that the overall payoff function $\omega$ is given by

$$\omega(a;x)=\psi(\omega_1(a;x),\ldots,\omega_n(a;x)) \tag{1.14}$$

through a certain function $\psi(\cdot)$ of $\omega_1,\ldots,\omega_n$; and 2) $\eta$ assigns the information structure $\eta_i$ to $D_i$, $i=1,\ldots,n$.

In this case too, a N.e. decision rule corresponding to a given command $\gamma=(\zeta,\eta)$ and to the optimal command is defined as above.

Remark Here we shall remark upon the relation between our approach to the two level hierarchical organization, and that of Mesarovic et. al. [2]. First of all, in their approach, the essential results apply only to the deterministic cases. Accordingly, in them the information structure about the state of nature and about the decision rules are not considered. It is assumed (describing in our terminology) that the payoff to the inferior decision unit $D_i$ when $D_0$ orders a command $\gamma$ and $D_i$ chooses the actions $a_i$, $i=1,\ldots,n$, is given by

$$\omega_i(a_i,u_i|\gamma) \ , \tag{1.15}$$

where

$$u_i=K_i(a) \ , \tag{1.16}$$

and $K_i(\cdot)$ is the given function of $a=(a_1,\ldots,a_n)$ called the interaction function. The overall payoff to the organization is assumed to be given by

$$\omega(a|\gamma)=\psi(\omega_1(a_1,u_1|\gamma),\ldots,\omega_n(a_n,u_n|\gamma)) \ , \tag{1.17}$$

where $\psi(\bullet)$ is a specified function. Now just because of the calculation, assuming that $D_i$ can control both $a_i$ and $u_i$, let $\bar{a}_i(\gamma)$, $\bar{u}_i(\gamma)$ be such that

$$\max_{a_i,u_i} \omega_i(a_i,u_i|\gamma)=\omega_i(\bar{a}_i(\gamma),\bar{u}_i(\gamma)|\gamma) \ . \tag{1.18}$$

If it happens that

$$\bar{u}_i(\gamma)=K_i(\bar{a}(\gamma)) \ , \quad i=1,\ldots,n \ , \tag{1.19}$$

then Mesarovic says <u>interaction balance</u> (i.b.) holds for $\bar{a}(\gamma)=(\bar{a}_1(\gamma),\ldots,\bar{a}_n(\gamma))$ under a command $\gamma$. And it is assumed that all the inferior decision units $D_i$, $i=1,\ldots,n$ are satisfied with $\bar{a}(\gamma)$. Let $\Gamma^*$ be the set of all commands $\gamma\varepsilon\Gamma$ under which there exists an action $\bar{a}(\gamma)$ for which i.b. holds. If $\gamma^*\varepsilon\Gamma^*$ exists such that

$$\omega(\bar{a}(\gamma^*)|\gamma^*)=\max_{\gamma\varepsilon\Gamma^*} \omega(\bar{a}(\gamma)|\gamma) \ , \tag{1.20}$$

then $\gamma^*$ is called an optimal command.

If, under a command $\gamma\varepsilon\Gamma^*$, i.b. holds for $\bar{a}(\gamma)$, then it is clear that $\bar{a}(\gamma)$ is N.e., assuming of course, $\omega_i$ is given by (1.15) and by (1.16). But it is also clear that for a N.e. action $\hat{a}(\gamma)$, i.b. does not necessarily hold. In these senses, it may be said that our approach is more general than that of Mesarovic. But it will be shown later (in § 3) that in order to obtain a solution in our approach we will have to assume something more.

## 2. An Example in Case I

We shall borrow Marschak's example [1] and modify it to our case. There are two inferior decision units $D_E$ and $D_W$. They must decide whether to accept the offered price in the east or in the west. Their possible actions are $a_E=1$, $a_E=0$ and $a_W=1$, $a_W=0$, where $a_E=1(0)$ means that $D_E$ accepts (does not accept) the offered price in the east, and $a_W$ is analogously defined. If the inferior decision unit accepts the offer, then a certain machine must be manufactured either in factory $F_1$ or in factory $F_2$. When the offered price is p and the manufacturing cost is c, then the profit to the inferior decision unit is p-c. The offered price will be denoted by $p_E$ and $p_W$ respectively in the east and in the west. The manufacturing cost by $F_i$ is $c_i$, i=1,2. We assume

$$c_1=5 \ , \quad c_2=8 \ ,$$

and the common joint distribution $\phi$ of $p_E$ and $p_W$ to $D_o$, $D_E$ and $D_W$ is given by Table 2.1.

Table 2.1

| | | $p_W$: 12 | 3 | |
|---|---|---|---|---|
| $p_E$ | 10 | .60 | .15 | .75 |
| | 4 | .05 | .20 | .25 |
| | | .65 | .35 | 1.00 |

Now there is the superior decision unit $D_o$ which gives a command $\gamma$ to the inferior decision units $D_1$ and $D_2$. Let the possible information structures be as follows:

$\eta_o$: $D_E(D_W)$ must choose his action without knowing $p_E(p_W)$ ,

$\eta_1$: $D_E(D_W)$ can choose his action after knowing $p_E(p_W)$ .

Further let $\zeta_i$ be the following command by $D_o$:

$\zeta_1$: $D_E$ can use $F_1$ and $D_W$ can use $F_2$, but not conversely ,

$\zeta_2$: $D_E$ can use $F_2$ and $D_W$ can use $F_1$, but not conversely ,

$\zeta_1'$: $\zeta_1$, but if $D_E$ does not use $F_1$, then $D_W$ can use $F_1$ ,

$\zeta_2'$: $\zeta_2$, but if $D_W$ does not use $F_1$, then $D_E$ can use $F_1$ .

Combining these components, let the possible commands by $D_o$ be as follows:

$$\gamma_1=(\eta_o,\zeta_1),\ \gamma_2=(\eta_o,\zeta_2),\ \gamma_3=(\eta_o,\zeta_1'),\ \gamma_4=(\eta_o,\zeta_2');$$
$$\gamma_5=(\eta_1,\zeta_1),\ \gamma_6=(\eta_1,\zeta_2),\ \gamma_7=(\eta_1,\zeta_1'),\ \gamma_8=(\eta_1,\zeta_2') \ . \qquad (2.1)$$

It is easily seen that the profit function $\omega_i$ for $D_i$ (where i=1,2 refers to E,W respectively) is given as follows ($c_1 < c_2$):

$$\begin{cases}\omega_1(a_E=1,a_W,p_E,p_W|\zeta_1)=p_E-c_1, \text{ for all } a_W \text{ and } p_W\\ \omega_2(a_E,a_W=1,p_E,p_W|\zeta_2)=p_W-c_2, \text{ for all } a_E \text{ and } p_E\end{cases}$$
$$\begin{cases}\omega_1(a_E=1,a_W,p_E,p_W|\zeta_2)=p_E-c_2, \text{ for all } a_W \text{ and } p_W\\ \omega_2(a_E,a_W=1,p_E,p_W|\zeta_2)=p_W-c_1, \text{ for all } a_E \text{ and } p_E\end{cases}$$
$$\begin{cases}\omega_1(a_E=1,a_W,p_E,p_W|\zeta_1')=p_E-c_1, \text{ for all } a_W \text{ and } p_W\\ \omega_2(a_E,a_W=1,p_E,p_W|\zeta_1')=\begin{cases}p_W-c_2, \text{ for } a_E=1 \text{ and all } p_E\\ p_W-c_1, \text{ for } a_E=0 \text{ and all } p_E\end{cases}\end{cases}$$
$$\begin{cases}\omega_1(a_E=1,a_W,p_E,pW|\zeta_2')=\begin{cases}p_E-c_2, \text{ for } a_W=1 \text{ and all } p_W\\ p_E-c_1, \text{ for } a_W=0 \text{ and all } p_W\end{cases}\\ \omega_2(a_E,a_W=1,p_E,p_W|\zeta_2')=p_W-c_1, \text{ for all } a_E \text{ and } p_E\end{cases}$$

In all cases, the value of $\omega_1(\omega_2)$ for $a_E=0(a_W=0)$ is 0.

Let the overall profit $\omega$ be given by

$$\omega=\omega_1+\omega_2 \ . \qquad (2.2)$$

Then denoting the maximum expected profit for the inferior decision unit $D_i$ under a command $\gamma$ by $\Omega_i(\gamma)$, the maximum expected profit when a command is $\gamma$ is given by

$$\Omega(\gamma)=\Omega_1(\gamma)+\Omega_2(\gamma) \ . \qquad (2.3)$$

We may easily calculate the following results:

$$\Omega_1(\gamma_2)=\Omega_1(\gamma_4)=0.50,\ \Omega_1(\gamma_6)=1.50,\ \Omega_1(\gamma_8)=1.95 \ ,$$
$$\Omega_1(\gamma_1)=\Omega_1(\gamma_3)=3.50,\ \Omega_1(\gamma_5)=\Omega_1(\gamma_7)=3.75 \ ; \qquad (2.4)$$
$$\Omega_2(\gamma_1)=\Omega_2(\gamma_3)=0.85,\ \Omega_2(\gamma_5)=2.60,\ \Omega_2(\gamma_7)=2.75 \ ,$$
$$\Omega_2(\gamma_2)=\Omega_2(\gamma_4)=3.85,\ \Omega_2(\gamma_6)=\Omega_2(\gamma_8)=4.55 \ ; \qquad (2.5)$$

and

$$\Omega(\gamma_1)=\Omega(\gamma_2)=\Omega(\gamma_3)=\Omega(\gamma_4)=4.35\ ,$$

$$\Omega(\gamma_6)=6.05,\ \Omega(\gamma_5)=6.35,\ \Omega(\gamma_7)=\Omega(\gamma_8)=6.50 \qquad (2.6)$$

Thus, if we disregard the information cost, we then have the following conclusion: the optimal command $\gamma^o$ by $D_o$ is $\gamma_7=(\eta_1,\zeta_1')$ or $\gamma_8=(\eta_1,\zeta_2')$. Under the command $\gamma^o=\gamma_7(\gamma_8)$, $D_E$ and $D_W$ are satisfied with the expected profit 3.75 (1.95) and 2.75 (4.55) respectively, and the organization is satisfied by obtaining the maximum expected profit of 6.50.

## 3. Some Examples in Case II

Before taking up examples in Case II, we shall state the following proposition which applies both in Case I and II.

Proposition 1. If the objective function $\omega_i(a_1,\ldots,a_n;x)$ assigned to the inferior decision unit $D_i$ is differentiable with respect to each $a_j$ for any fixed value of $x\varepsilon X$, then a N.e. decision rule $\hat{\alpha}=(\hat{\alpha}_1,\ldots,\hat{\alpha}_n)$ under the information structure $\eta=(\eta_1,\ldots,\eta_n)$ is given as follows. Let

$$\psi_i(a_i,y_i)=E\{\overline{\omega}_i(\hat{\alpha}_1(y_1),\ldots,a_i,\ldots,\hat{\alpha}_n(y_n);y_1,\ldots,y_n)|y_i\}, \quad (3.1)$$

where

$$\overline{\omega}_i(a_1,\ldots,a_n;y_1,\ldots,y_n)=E\{\omega_i(a;x)|y_1,\ldots,y_n)\},\ i=1,\ldots,n \quad (3.2)$$

Then $\hat{\alpha}$ can be determined as the solution of the following simultaneous equation

$$\left.\frac{\partial\psi i}{\partial a_i}\right|_{a_i=\hat{\alpha}_i(y_i)} =0,\quad i=1,\ldots,n\ . \qquad (3.3)$$

(For proof, refer to Marschak and Radner [1].)

Now in applying Proposition 1 for obtaining a N.e. decision rule, we face a difficulty. Because without assuming something such as the following Assumption 1 or 2, any decision unit $D_i$ will not be able to know the simultaneous equation (3.3) and much less solve it by himself.

Assumption 1 (Computing Center). All the inferior decision units $D_i$, $i=1,\dots,n$ transmit their equations (3.3) to a certain computing center and it can solve the simultaneous equation (3.3) for $\hat{\alpha}=(\hat{\alpha}_1,\dots,\hat{\alpha}_n)$ and send back $\hat{\alpha}_i$ to $D_i$, $i=1,\dots,n$.

Assumption 2 (Communication). Each inferior decision unit $D_i$ communicates his prior probability law $\phi_i$ and his objective function $\omega_i$ to all other inferior decision units $D_j$, $j\neq i$.

Example 1. There are two inferior decision units $D_1$, $D_2$. The overall payoff function is given beforehand by

$$\omega(a_1,a_2;x_1,x_2)=-a_1^2-a_2^2+2qa_1a_2-a_1x_1-a_2x_2\ , \tag{3.4}$$

where $-1<q<1$.

Let the command $\gamma_o=(\zeta_o,\eta_o)$ by the superior decision unit $D_o$ be as follows:

1) $\zeta_o$ assigns the following payoff function $\omega_i$ to $D_i$:

$$\omega_1(a_1,a_2;x_1,x_2)=-a_1^2+qa_1a_2-a_1x_1\ , \tag{3.5}$$

$$\omega_2(a_1,a_2;x_1,x_2)=-a_2^2+qa_1a_2-a_2x_2\ . \tag{3.6}$$

Then it is clear that

$$\omega=\omega_1+\omega_2$$

2) $\gamma_o$ assigns the null information structure $\eta_o$ to each $D_i$, i.e., $D_i$, must choose $a_i$ without having any information concerning $x_1$, $x_2$, except his prior probability law $\phi_i$, $i=1,2$.

Under the command $\gamma_o$, each decision unit $D_i$, $i=1,2$ is concerned with

$$\begin{aligned}\overline{\omega}_1(a_1,a_2)&=E_{\phi_1}\{\omega_1(a_1,a_2;x_1,x_2)\}\\&=-a_1^2+qa_1a_2-a_1\mu_1'\ ,\end{aligned} \tag{3.7}$$

$$\overline{\omega}_2(a_1,a_2)=E_{\phi_2}\{\omega_2(a_1,a_2;x_1,x_2)\}$$
$$=-a_2^2+qa_1a_2-a_2\mu_2' \ , \qquad (3.8)$$

where

$$\mu_i'=E_{\phi_i}\{x_i\} \ , \quad i=1,2 \ .$$

Then the equation (3.3) becomes to

$$\frac{\partial\overline{\omega}_1}{\partial a_1} = -2a_1+qa_2-\mu_1'=0 \ , \qquad (3.9)$$

$$\frac{\partial\overline{\omega}_2}{\partial a_2} = -2a_2+qa_1-\mu_2'=0 \ . \qquad (3.10)$$

Solving the equation (3.9) and (3.10) for a N.e. action $\hat{a}=(\hat{a}_1,\hat{a}_2)$, we have

$$\hat{a}_1=\frac{2\mu_1'+q\mu_2'}{q^2-4} \ , \quad \hat{a}_2=\frac{2\mu_2'+q\mu_1'}{q^2-4} \qquad (3.11)$$

In order to $D_i$ knows $a_i$, i=1,2, we will have to assume Assumption 1 or 2.

Now let us assume that under the null information structure $\eta_o$, the superior decision unit $D_o$, in a centralized way, calculates the values $a_1^*$ and $a_2^*$ of $a_1$ and $a_2$ which maximize the overall expected payoff function

$$\overline{\omega}(a_1,a_2)\equiv E_{\phi_o}\{\omega(a_1,a_2;x_1,x_2)\}$$
$$=-a_1^2-a_2^2+2qa_1a_2-a_1\mu_1-a_2\mu_2 \qquad (3.12)$$

where $\mu_i=E_{\phi_o}\{x_i\}$, i=1,2,

and orders $D_1$ and $D_2$ to take the actions $a_1^*$ and $a_2^*$ respectively.

Now it is easy to know that

$$a_1^*=\frac{\mu_1+q\mu_2}{2(q^2-1)} \ , \quad a_2^*=\frac{q\mu_1+\mu_2}{2(q^2-1)} \qquad (3.13)$$

It should be noted that $(a_1^*,a_2^*)$ is different from $(\hat{a}_1,\hat{a}_2)$ given by (3.11), even if $\mu_i'=\mu_i$, except for the case of $\mu_i'=\mu_i=0$, i=1,2. Although under the command $\gamma^o=(\zeta_o,\eta_o)$, $(\hat{a}_1,\hat{a}_2)$ given by (3.11) is a N.e. solution for $D_1,D_2$, it does not give the maximum possible value to the overall expected payoff $\hat{\omega}$ given by (3.12). Thus, when $\eta_o$ is fixed, $\gamma_o=(\zeta_o,\eta_o)$ will not be an optimal command and in fact not, as is seen later.

When the overall payoff function $\omega(a_1,\dots,a_n;x)$ is given beforehand, i.e. in Case II, we have the following

<u>Proposition 2</u>. In a two-level hierarchical organization consisting of the superior decision unit $D_o$ and the inferior decision units $D_i$, i=1, ...,n: 1) if the overall payoff function $\omega(a_1,\dots,a_n;x)$ which is given beforehand is and differentiable with respect to $a_i$, i=1,...,n for each fixed $x\varepsilon X$, 2) if the information structure $\eta_i$ to be assigned to $D_i$ is already fixed, i=1,...,n, 3) if the prior probability law on X is the same function $\phi$ for all the members i=0,1,...,n, and 4) if any objective function $\omega_i(a_1,\dots,a_n;x)$ could be assigned to $D_i$, i=1,...,n, then we have: (1) the optimal command $\gamma^*=(\zeta^*,\eta)$ by $D_o$, where $\eta=(\eta_1,\dots,\eta_n)$ is the fixed information structure, is given by taking $\zeta^*$ as follows. The component $\zeta^*$ of the command $\gamma^*$ assigns the function $\beta_i\omega$ as the objective function $\omega_i^*$ of $D_i$, i.e., $\omega_i^*=\beta_i\omega$, i=1,...,n, where $\beta_i$ are any real numbers such that $\beta_i\geq 0$, $\Sigma\beta_i=1$, and (2) each inferior decision unit $D_i$ can obtain a N.e. decision rule by himself without relying or Assumption 1 or 2.

<u>Proof</u>. It is clear that

$$\omega=\sum_i\omega_i^* \ . \tag{3.14}$$

Now let

$$\begin{aligned}\overline{\omega}_i^*(a_1,\dots,a_n;y_1,\dots,y_n)&\equiv E\{\omega_i^*(a_1,\dots,a_n;x)|y_1,\dots,y_n\}\\ &=\beta_i\overline{\omega}(a_1,\dots,a_n;y_1,\dots,y_n)\ , \end{aligned}\tag{3.15}$$

Where $y_i = \eta_i(x), x \varepsilon X$ and

$$\overline{\omega}(a_1,\dots,a_n;y_1,\dots,y_n) \equiv E\{\omega(a_1,\dots,a_n;x)|y_1,\dots,y_n\} \ . \quad (3.16)$$

For the N.e. decision rule $\hat{\alpha}=(\hat{\alpha}_1,\dots,\hat{\alpha}_n)$, let

$$\psi_i(a_i,y_i)=E\{\overline{\omega}_i^*(\hat{\alpha}_1(y_1),\dots,a_i,\dots,\hat{\alpha}_n(y_n);y_1,\dots,y_n)|y_i\}, \quad (3.17)$$

and

$$\psi(a_i,y_i)=E\{\overline{\omega}(\hat{\alpha}_1 y_1),\dots,a_i,\dots,\hat{\alpha}_n(y_n);y_1,\dots,y_n)|y_i\} \ , \quad (3.18)$$

$$i=1,\dots,n \ .$$

Then from (3.15)-(3.18), it is clear that

$$\psi_i(a_i,y_i)=\beta_i\psi(a_i,y_i) \ , \quad i=1,\dots,n \ . \quad (3.19)$$

Therefore by (3.19), the simultaneous equation

$$\left.\frac{\partial\psi_i}{\partial a_i}\right|_{a_i=\hat{\alpha}_i(y_i)} =0, \quad i=1,\dots,n \ , \quad (3.20)$$

which determines the N.e. decision rule $\hat{\alpha}=(\hat{\alpha}_1,\dots,\hat{\alpha}_n)$ under the command $\gamma^*$, is equivalent to the simultaneous equation

$$\left.\frac{\partial\psi}{\partial a_i}\right|_{a_i=\alpha_i^*(y_i)} =0 \ , \quad i=1,\dots,n \ , \quad (3.21)$$

which determines the p.b.p.s. decision rule $\alpha^*$ of the team having $\omega$ as its objective function and in this case $\alpha^*$ attains the maximum expected payoff of $\omega$ under the given information structure $\eta$. Therefore under the command $\gamma^*=(\zeta^*,\eta)$, the N.e. decision rule given by (3.20) attains the maximum possible value of the overall expected payoff. This means that $\gamma^*$ is the optimal command by $D_0$, insofar as the information structure is fixed as $\eta$. Further because of (3.19), for each i, the simultaneous equation (3.20) is equivalent to

$$\left.\frac{\partial\psi_i}{\partial a_j}\right|_{a_j=\hat{\alpha}_j(y_j)} =0, \quad j-1,\dots,n. \quad (3.21)$$

So, in this case, each inferior decision unit $D_i$ can find out his own N.e. decision rule by himself without relying on other assumptions. q.e.d.

We should remark that this approach has a serious difficulty in application. Because the inferior decision unit $D_i$, i=1,2 will have its own specific restricted operational capacity. But Proposition 2, neglecting this fact, assumes that $D_i$ could be assigned any objective function $\omega_i$, i=1,2.

Example 2. In Example 1 assuming that $\phi_0=\phi_1=\phi_2$, let the command by $D_0$ be $\gamma_0^*=(\zeta^*,\eta_0)$, where $\zeta^*$ assigns the inferior decision unit $D_i$ the following payoff function $\omega_i^*$

$$\omega_1^*=\beta_1\omega \;, \quad \omega_2^*=\beta_2\omega \;, \tag{3.22}$$

and where $\beta_i$ are any fixed real numbers such that

$$\beta_1,\beta_2>0 \;, \quad \beta_1+\beta_2=1 \;. \tag{3.23}$$

Then it is clear that

$$\omega=\omega_1^*+\omega_2^* \;, \tag{3.24}$$

and

$$\begin{aligned}\overline{\omega}_i^*(a_1,a_2)&=E\{\omega_i^*(a_1,a_2;x_1,x_2)\}\\&=\beta_i\overline{\omega} \;,\end{aligned} \tag{3.25}$$

where $\overline{\omega}$ is given by (3.12). Therefore by (3.25), under the command $\gamma^*$, the simultaneous equation

$$\frac{\partial\overline{\omega}_i^*}{\partial a_i}=0 \;, \quad i=1,2 \;, \tag{3.26}$$

which gives the N.e. solution, is equivalent to each of the simultaneous equations

$$\frac{\partial\overline{\omega}_i^*}{\partial a_1}=0 \;, \quad \frac{\partial\overline{\omega}_1^*}{\partial a_2}=0 \;, \tag{3.27}$$

and

$$\frac{\partial\bar{\omega}_2^*}{\partial a_1}=0 \ , \quad \frac{\partial\bar{\omega}_2^*}{\partial a_2}=0 \ . \tag{3.28}$$

This means that each inferior decision unit $D_i$, i=1,2 can discover the N.e. solution under the optimal command $\gamma^*$ without relying upon Assumption 1 or 2. This also means that in this case the organization is coordinable by i.b. principle under the command $\gamma^*$ in Mesarovic's sense.

Example 3. In Example 1 assuming $\phi_0=\phi_1=\phi_2$, let the information structure to be assigned to the inferior decision units $D_i$, i=1,2 be fixed as any one $\eta=(\eta_1,\eta_2)$. Further, let the command $\gamma^*$ by $D_0$ be $\gamma^*=(\zeta^*,\eta)$, where $\zeta^*$ is defined as in Example 2. Then we easily see that the simultaneous equation (3.20), which gives the N.e. decision rule $\hat{\alpha}=(\hat{\alpha}_1,\hat{\alpha}_2)$, is given by

$$\begin{cases} \hat{\alpha}_1(y_1)+\frac{1}{2}k_1(y_1)=qE\{\hat{\alpha}_2(y_2)|y_1\} & (3.29) \\ \hat{\alpha}_2(y_2)+\frac{1}{2}k_2(y_2)=qE\{\hat{\alpha}_1(y_1)|y_2\}, & (3.30) \end{cases}$$

where $y_i=\eta_i(x)$, $x\varepsilon X$ and

$$k_i(y_i)=E\{x_i|y_i\} \ , \quad i=1,2. \tag{3.31}$$

As an illustration, if we further assume that the information structure $\eta=(\eta_1,\eta_2)$ is such that $y_1=\eta_1(x)$ and $y_2=\eta_2(x)$, $x\varepsilon X$ are statistically independent. For example, $x=(x_1,x_2)$ and $\eta_1(x)=x_1$, $\eta_2(x)=x_2$ and $x_1$ and $x_2$ are independent. Then the equations (3.29) and (3.30) become

$$\hat{\alpha}_1(y_1)+\frac{1}{2}k_1(y_1)=qE\{\hat{\alpha}_2(y_2)\} \ , \tag{3.32}$$

$$\hat{\alpha}_2(y_2)+\frac{1}{2}k_2(y_2)=qE\{\hat{\alpha}_1(y_1)\} \ . \tag{3.33}$$

Taking the expected value of the both sides of (3.33) with respect to $y_2$, we have

$$E\{\hat{\alpha}_2(y_2)\}=-\frac{1}{2}\mu_2+qE\{\hat{\alpha}_1(y_1)\} \ . \tag{3.34}$$

Substituting (3.34) in (3.32), we have

$$\hat{\alpha}_1(y_1)-q^2E\{\hat{\alpha}_1(y_1)\}+\frac{1}{2}k_1(y_1)+\frac{1}{2}q\mu_2=0 \ . \tag{3.35}$$

Thus the inferior decision unit $D_1$ will be able to solve the equation (3.35) by himself. For $D_2$ the situation is analogous.

Remark So far we have always been assuming that the information structure $\eta$ is fixed. The problem of choosing an information structure will have to be investigated in this approach.

## References

[1] Marschak, J. and R. Radner, Economic Theory of Teams, Cowles Foundation Monograph 22 (1972).

[2] Mesarovic, M.D. Macko, and Takahara, Theory of Hierarchical, Multi-level Systems, Academic Press (1970).

# INTEGRATION OF THE BUDGET AND STANDARD COST SYSTEM IN MANAGEMENT ACCOUNTING

Kazuo Mizoguchi

Budgeting and standard cost accounting are two of the most important tools in modern management. These two tools must be integrated in order to have a complete control system. Therefore, if we intend to combine them successfully, we need to understand the functional and systematic relation between them.

In the United States, the uses of budgets and standard costs have been important sources of management control for decades. Management accounting has developed a strong foundation not only in the literature but also in practice. It is evident that standard cost accounting has been strongly influenced by scientific management from an engineering perspective. On the other hand, budgetary control is based on accounting thought. Given the different origins of standard cost accounting and budgeting, can these two control systems work in an integrated way? It is also important to note that budgetary control depends on and is oriented to the concept of period profit planning as has been widely discussed in Japan in the last decade.

In Japan, it is acceptable theory that the budget system has three fundamental functions in management: planning, coordination, and control. The planning function of the budget is mainly understood as the process of budgeting with two different dimensions. The first one is short-range business planning, and the second is the setting of departmental objectives. The latter is divided into the individual responsibilities of decentralized management levels, and the role of the control function of the budget is realized through it. These two meanings have not been clearly examined by academics and especially by practitioners. With rapid technological development, the planning process becomes more important as a tool of business policy and less important as a part of the budgeting process.

Consequently, the function of the budget must be independent of planning and limited to the coordination and control functions of departments. In addition, we need to look at the differences and relationship between budgeting and standard cost accounting as control devices.

Obviously, budgeting includes the total operations of an organization, not just the aspect of cost. In so far as the budget deals with cost figures, however, there arises a problem of integrating budgetary control and cost control by standard cost accounting.

Many authors have already pointed out that budgetary control contains cost control, and cost control in Japanese practice is very often performed on the basis of budgetary control. But that is mostly due to the fact that standard cost accounting is not well developed in Japan. Assume that the function of standard cost accounting is cost control narrowly defined. Then, it is conceivable that the function of cost control, which is often accomplished through budgets, could be accomplished by standard costing in order to unify the areas of cost control more systematically.

A quantitative control of the cost elements is at the heart of cost control. Recently, the main function of budgeting has shifted from cost control to short-range profit planning of a decentralized organization. In this concept, the activities in various areas of responsibilities of the business are derived from the profit plan.

Budgets are normally concerned with time periods, whereas standard cost accounting is normally concerned with units. This distinction is important in understanding the difference between budgeting and standard cost accounting with respect to the spending control of materials and labor.

But it is not meant that control by budgeting is accomplished only in the form of accounting for periods. For instance, the capture of sales by individual items is not necessarily in a process of execution of the sales budget. It may be explained that the control of an individual item should be delivered to the standard costing as cost control of the consumed materials and labor, for it is more suitable for controlling them than the budget.

In return, the budget keeps the sales control, in which no difficulty exists. The following scheme illustrates more specifically the relationship between budgeting and standard cost accounting. It can be generally said that cost control is accomplished by comparing standard and actual costs and by the analysis of variances in order to determine why these variances exist. The individual departments are responsibility centers, with the cost center as an economic unit that can be considered as an origin of profit.

The cost center is responsible for all costs incurred by that center. In the area of cost accounting, cost control is performed for direct and indirect costs. Indirect costs tend to be viewed on a much broader perspective than are direct costs. From the economic viewpoint, indirect costs are normally controlled for an aggregate of cost centers rather than for an individual center. These indirect costs are principally controlled by budgets rather than standard costs, and the major reason for that is that indirect costs do not provide useful information for cost control when they become a part of cost variances per unit of product.

Even if the cost variances of indirect cost for the product were identified, a departmental head could find no way to correct the unfavorable variance. Therefore, indirect costs should be controlled in their total amount for each department. The cost variances for indirect costs are classified and analyzed into two or three subvariances according to their different origins.

By using the three-variance method, the variances are divided into the budget, efficiency and volume variances. The accounting method in this case seems to belong to standard cost accounting. But their control itself is accomplished through budget variance through the budget system.

From such a standpoint, the relationship between the budget system and standard cost accounting mentioned above must be corrected to some extent. For the control of indirect costs the budget still has its cost control function. In addition, the direct cost control is accomplished by standard cost accounting. Naturally the cost control of direct costs plays an essential role in its narrow meaning. At the same time, it should be considered that the fundamental task of modern budgetary contro is not in a tight and one-sided cost control but in a total control of the whole business. With regard to indirect cost control, it was only shown that the budget and standard cost accounting are related to each other.

On the basis of the above discussion, the relationship between the budget and standard cost accounting is explained in the following illustration.

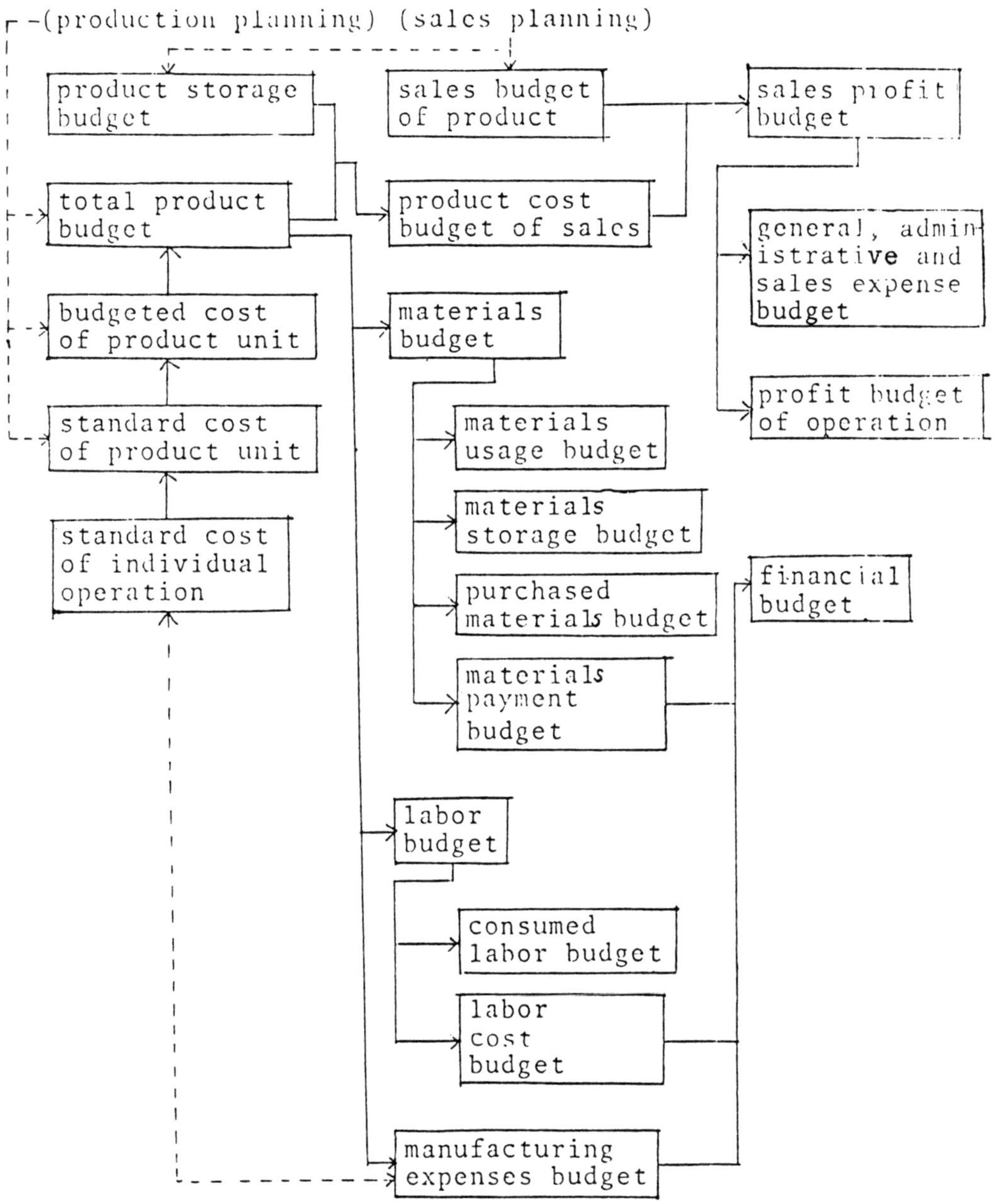
(production planning) (sales planning)
product storage budget
sales budget of product
sales profit budget
total product budget
product cost budget of sales
general, administrative and sales expense budget
budgeted cost of product unit
materials budget
profit budget of operation
standard cost of product unit
materials usage budget
standard cost of individual operation
materials storage budget
purchased materials budget
financial budget
materials payment budget
labor budget
consumed labor budget
labor cost budget
manufacturing expenses budget

This illustration should support the discussion we have made thus far. The dotted line between the "manufacturing expenses budget" and "standard cost of individual operation" means finding out the standardized costs per unit and also setting up the manufacturing expenses budget. Furthermore, the standard costs of each individual operation and the standard cost of a product unit are related to each other, and they are dependent on the product plan. This product plan has already been set up as a component of the total period plan and consequently forms a starting point for budgeting. Indeed, management calculates in advance the past cost of the finished goods and brings it forward as an element in the total profit plan. But the basis for establishing both the standard cost and the budget costs should be taken from the product plan developed by top-management. The amount of standard cost in addition to budget cost generally depends on the respective product plans, in so far as a realizable standard is under consideration. The contents of the product plan are dependent on the type of production.

But it is especially important to ask if the product plan of each individual operation is derived from the overall production plan. Each individual product plan is dependent on the standard and budget cost per unit, and these product plans must be linked together in a logical way. An important element in this process is the manufacturing expenses budget by product line.

By budget, the author means the total amount of the budgeted costs by type of finished goods, which is composed of the budgeted cost ratios of the individual products multiplied by the volume of planned production.

In addition, let us ask how to measure the budgeted costs per unit of the product on the basis of standard cost. The budgeted cost of finished goods is generally derived by the standard cost. However, a difference usually arises between the budgeted and standard cost which we shall term a necessary allowance. This necessary allowance is the link between the two systems. The "total manufacturing cost budget" by product is located above the "budgeted cost of product unit" in the above schematic illustration. The budgeted cost per unit multiplied by the volume of product according to the production plan are, as already explained, the total budgeted costs for the specific period.

However, note that the budget of manufacturing costs, which can also be called the total product budget should be broken down into the various budgets for materials, labor, and manufacturing expenses, which do not depend on the types of finished goods. The "materials budget" further consists of four components. Those are "materials usage budget," "materials stock budget," "materials purchase budget," and "materials payment budget."

Now the author would like to try to determine if the material usage budget could serve as a cost control. For simplicity, let's assume that the material usage budget is only for the direct material cost. This budget is determined by dividing it into the different kinds of material. In the above situation where the standard cost system is not well developed, the material usage budget should be used to control materials usage. But the materials are not totally controlled in this case. Since control through the budget is so inaccurate, one can not exactly know why a materials usage variance exists, not find a way to correct it. Therefore, if modern standard cost accounting is introduced, the materials usage budget is better able to perform its function of cost control.

The primary function of the materials usage budget can be found elsewhere, namely in the situation where it forms the basic record of the materials purchase budget. The materials usage budget is determined on the basis of both the production plan and the budgeted cost information per units of product and is divided into different classes of materials. The "materials payment budget" is always a part of the financial budgets.

Consequently, the fundamental role of the today's material budgets lies not in the control of the materials used, but in the control of the purchase and payment of materials.

The "labor budget" matches the "labor cost budget" which is exactly like the materials usage budget in the context of the materials budget. But the role of the "labor cost budget" is different from the materials usage budget. Labor costs are always fixed in Japan, for they are dependent not on efficiency but rather on labor hours. Under such a situation, labor costs generally have the characteristics of fixed costs, and consequently it is not as useful to control this cost through a cost accounting.

Controlling labor cost through the budget is not important either. The use of budget and standard cost accounting is relevant from the standpoint of top management. The labor hours of individual operations, just as of cost centers, are controlled through standard costs, and unfavorable variances can be traced directly to specific operations. This control each period through the standard cost system can reduce the unfavorable labor cost variance. But labor cost reduction in a system of lifetime employment depends upon the decision of top management, for the standard cost system merely provides information. When one says that total labor costs are fixed costs, it is implied that total control is through the budget system, i.e. the comparison of standard with actual cost.

Once again, the correlation between the function of the budget and the standard cost system becomes important. The manufacturing expenses budget in the illustration forms the foundation of the measurement of the standard manufacturing cost per product and operation. This budget is incorporated into the standard cost system. However, the analysis of the manufacturing cost variance should accomplish the cost control with the individual responsibility and authority of each operation, not through the standard cost system but through the manufacturing expenses budget of each operation. One can understand the control function of the budget in its limited sphere.

Now let us consider the other side of the budgetary control, mainly the control of the output. As is shown in the illustration presented previously, the sales profit budget by product is derived from the manufacturing cost, inventory, and sales budgets by product, and the general administrative and sales expense budget for the respective accounting periods. This combined system, which is originally limited to the period profit plan and is then diverted to the sales profit budget, plays the role of the profit control. The function of the modern budget system would be complete if the system were combined with the financial budget. The cost budget, which is included in the sales profit budget, contains the budgeted cost by individual operation, and the budgeted cost can be found through the standard cost system.

In the above discussion, the relationship between budgetary control and the standard cost system was generally explained. Many authors discuss the budget only from the perspective of cost control. In the model illustrated and discussed above, however, the budgeted cost per product unit does not play any important role for cost control if standard cost is used in addition to the budgeted cost and if the periodic income determination, namely the profit control of the output, is made. In the chemical industry in Japan, it can easily be seen that the tightness of the budgeted cost and that of the standard cost are in accord with each other. One can use these normalized costs for both profit and cost controls. Because of the unique production process, however, like the relationship between raw materials and manufactured products in the pharmaceutical industry, the definite chemical effect is constant, and the significance of the cost control itself is smaller than in other businesses such as in the machinery, electric, and automobile industries.

However, the difference between budgeted costs and standard costs can be found in other cases. This difference comes from the material usage and the labor productivity, i.e. from the two cost standards. The budgeted cost should coincide with those amounts that show the allowable labor productivity. Strictly speaking, however, such a budgeted cost of the individual product is not so appropriate for the cost control. Therefore, one must combine the two control systems to yield the following:

Standard cost + Planning allowance = Budgeted cost

In conclusion, it is emphasized that the budget system with the standard cost system must be understood not as the one side of the cost control but the cost and profit control in their combined form.

# A GOAL-VECTOR APPROACH TO MULTIPLE OBJECTIVE CORPORATE PLANNING*

by

Tamio Fushimi

This paper presents a practical model for a multi-objective, multi-period corporate planning. A deviation-balancing approach based on a goal-vector concept is applied to a "model" corporation in Japan. However, the events and numerical data of the model corporation are greatly simplified so that the whole structure of the model can easily be envisioned, for the author's main concern is not to solve the current problem in an existing company but to present a typical example of multiple objective corporate planning.

The paper is divided into five sections: typical goals in corporate planning and characteristics of the goal activities; the essence of the goal-vector approach and an L-shaped model (a type of deviation-balancing model); the physical, organizational, and financial situations of the model corporation at the beginning of the planning period; mathematical formulations for the model corporation including the equations for preparing planned income statements and balance sheets, goal constraints, and technical constraints; and the results of the computer solutions under the two assumptions of maintaining the existing production capacity and expanding the capacity.

*This is as abstract. The entire article title and publication source are "A Practical Model for Multiple Objective Corporate Financial Planning: A Deviation Balancing Goal-Vector Approach," Keio Engineering Reports, Vol. 30, No. 10, August 1977.

Multiple Objectives

Several sub-objectives have been identified after taking into consideration their applicability to mathematical formulation. They are:

i) To pay a proper amount of dividend in each fiscal period in order to maintain good relationships with current and future shareholders.

ii) To increase the net income after tax in each period, maintaining a favorable ratio thereof to the invested capital.

iii) To expand the sales of each group of products, taking into account a good balance between each product, for maintaining and improving the company's position in the market.

iv) To maintain a proper cash balance in each period in order to assure a good liquidity of funds.

v) To maintain good financial ratios among the assets, liabilities, equity, and income. This goal has been specified in the following four goals:

a) To maintain a proper rate of income on total assets.

b) To maintain a good ratio between current assets and current liabilities.

c) To maintain a good ratio of net worth to the total assets.

d) To maintain a proper balance between the total fixed assets and capital resources (long-term liabilities and net worth).

Note: In actual corporate plans and various "non-financial" objectives, e.g., the consideration on product quality, employee welfare, and other organizational and environmental situations may be displayed. In this model, we regard these objectives as given conditions whose influences are reflected in planned fixed expenses and other financial parameters.

Characteristics of Goal Activities

The multiple goals of the model corporation, with the decisions confronted by the manager in the real world, suggest that we are dealing with the goal activities that have the following characteristics: (1) None of the goals have dominant priority over others where the ordering method of preemptive priority, which is widely used in traditional goal programming, can be applied; (2) it is seldom that the relationships between goals are substitutive enough to apply the weighting method, which is also widely used in traditional goal programming; (3) it is quite usual that a comprehensive corporate planning model is built for the purpose of monitoring future corporate situations over some periods, and the emphasis is placed upon a balance among the levels of performance in multiple periods for each goal item; (4) it is very hard to directly specify a tradeoff relationship among the multiple goals, but it is relatively easy for managers to specify a minimum required level for each goal, below which the managers do not want to allow the planned performance to go; (5) the level of performance in each goal that is presented in financial terms can usually be assumed to be continuously divisible between minimum required and sufficient levels; and (6) the list of goals and the minimum required and sufficient levels in each goal are not completely stable, since uncertainty is unavoidable. Therefore, it is desirable that the planning model is simple enough to allow many trial computations including the sensitivity analyses that deal with possible major changes of situations.

A Goal-Vector Approach

The characteristics of goal activities mentioned above suggest that a new pragmatic approach for building a comprehensive financial planning model is needed instead of applying goal programming techniques in the traditional way.

A goal-vector approach, which the author has developed for extending the applicability of multigoal programming to practical planning problems, is applied to the model corporation.

We consider an m-dimensional goal space composed of $g_i \geq 0, i=1,2, \cdots, m$, which represents the level of i-th goal. The level of performance in each goal is assumed to be linear function $g_i(x)=g_i(x_1,x_2,\cdots,x_n)$, $i=1,2,\cdots,m$, subject to linear constraints. When a minimum required level $g_i^o$ and a sufficient level $g_i^s$ are determined by a decision maker for each goal, a vector $\overrightarrow{G^oG^s}$ will be obtained by connecting two points $G^o=(g_1^o,g_2^o,\cdots,g_m^o)$ and $G^s=(g_1^s,g_2^s, \cdots, g_m^s)$ in the goal space. The vector $\overrightarrow{G^oG^s}$, which we call G-vector, is a useful indicator to show the direction of desirability of goal attainment.

A variety of utility functions associated with the G-vector can be defined. However, we have chosen the L-Shape Model illustrated below, which is a minimax utility function adjusted by the ratio of $\lambda_i=g_i^s-g_i^o$, $i=1,2\cdots m$.

L-Shape Model

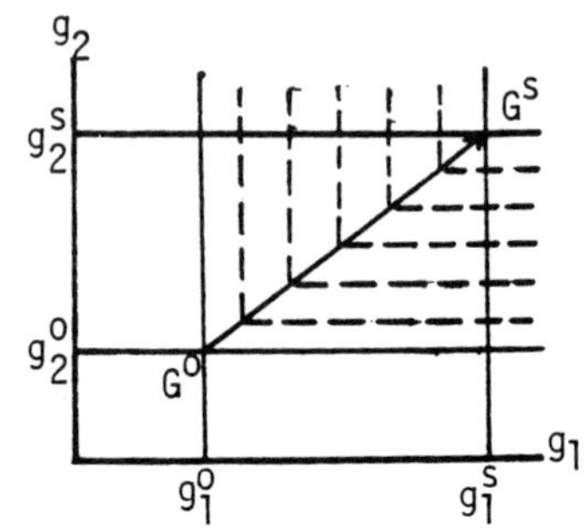

The reasons for the choice of this model are as follows: (1) Corporate executives usually wish to raise the level of planned performance in every goal, instead of assuming a preemptive priority for a sufficient substitutivity between goals, though considering a relative difference of importance among the goals. L-Shape utility function provides an easily understood projection of this goal-aiming process and usually brings about a better solution than the ordering and weighting models do; (2) the solution provides an improved ordering and continues to do this so long as possible, without overpowering anything else, in the same fashion as one achieves a Pareto optimum point; (3) its mathematical formulation and computation are simple enough to apply to practical corporate planning models.

Generally, we may regard the L-shaped function as a regret function in which the value of regret equals the difference between the sufficient level and what is actually attained for each goal. We represent it as an L-shape utility function, and then minimize the maximum regret value which is weighted by the ratio of $1/\lambda_i$, $i=1,2,\cdots,m$.

Thus adjusted regret R can be minimized by solving the following linear program:

(I) Minimize $y_1$

(II) Subject to

(a) $Ax+Iy-Iz=g^s$

(b) $y_i-\frac{\lambda_i}{\lambda_1}y_1=0$, $i=2,\cdots,m$

(c) $Ax\geq g^o$

(d) $Bx\leq L$

(e) $x,y,z\geq 0$,

where x is a column vector comprised of decision variables $x_j$, j = 1, 2, ..., n; y, z, $g^s$ and $g^o$ are column vectors comprised of $y_i$, $z_i$, $g_i^s$, i = 1, 2, ..., m, respectively; A and B are m x n and 1 x n matrices respectively; I is an m x m identity matrix. We call, for convenience, (a), (b), (c) above goal constraints, and (d) technical constraints, though the latter may include various "policy constraints" established by management. The deviation variables $d_i^- = g_i^s - g_i(x)$ and $d_i^+ = g_i(x) - g_i^s$, which are widely used in the usual goal programming, are obtained as:

(a) $y_i - z_i = d_i^-$ (when $y_i \geq z_i$)

(b) $z_i - y_i = d_i^+$ (when $y_i \leq z_i$).

<u>An Application of the Model</u>

As mentioned earlier, the model was tested by use of a computer run covering a four-year period of time under two different assumptions: top management would maintain the policy of holding the same production capacity as the initial condition through the planning period, making the necessary replacement of equipment; and top management would carefully expand production capacity. Before setting up a mathematical formulation of the model, it was necessary to make assumptions concerning the major departments of the company, the fixed assets, the labor force, the products and raw materials used, and revenue and cost estimations.

Once these conditions were set, 16 different decisions variables were defined and 48 parameters were set for each of the four years. The decision variables consisted of items such as the number of equipment to be invested at the beginning of each period, the quantity of each product to be produced each period, the quantity of each product to be sold in each period, the volume of raw materials to be purchased for each product in each period, and the amount of short-term and long-term borrowings to be made at the beginning of each period, the amount of securities to be purchased and sold in each period, and the amount of dividends to be paid at the end of each period. The parameters consisted of items such as the unit selling price of each product, the average labor cost per worker, depreciation charges, variable production costs per unit of each product, the cost per unit of each raw material, etc.

Once the decision variables and parameters were defined, the variables for the income statement and balance sheet each year were formulated mathematically. In the income statement, for example the total net sales for each period is obtained by multiplying the unit price by the quantity sold:

$$V_{1t}=a_{1t}X_{SAt}+a_{2t}X_{SBt}+a_{3t}X_{SCt}$$

where $V_{1t}$ is the total net sales in period t

$a_{1t},a_{2t},a_{3t}$ are the unit selling prices of products A, B, and C in period t

$X_{SAt},X_{SBt},X_{SCt}$ are the quantity of products A, B, and C sold in period t.

Similar equations are given for all variables in the balance sheet and income statement.

Once these relationships have been determined, the minimum required and sufficient levels for each goal are determined and then mathematically formulated. For example, the minimal required level of dividends is 8% of the capital stock, and the sufficient level is 20% of the capital stock. In order to finally run the program, technical constraints are also added. For example, the production hours in a particular department are limited to a certain number of hours per unit of equipment.

## Results

It was found through applying the model to the fictional company in the study that the goal vector approach, assuming the L-Shape utility (regret) function, is very useful for practically achieving a well-balanced goal attainment as compared with the traditional goal programming approach such as the ordering and weighting methods. Using the model, the decision analysts will be able to perform any other test runs assuming a variety of conditions of goals, expected changes in market conditions, expected changes in revenue and expense factors, and so forth.

# ON THE RELATIONSHIPS BETWEEN THE VALUE AND THE AMOUNT OF INFORMATION*

By Hiroyuki Itami

The purpose of this paper is to analyze the relationships between the value of information provided by an information system and the amount of information provided by an information system. The value is essentially defined as the expected increase of utility by having an information system and the amount is defined as the expected decrease of the degree of uncertainty of the states of nature, the degree of uncertainty of a probability distribution being measured by entropy.

Investigations in this paper are particularly concerned with the "consistency" of the rankings of information systems by the value and by the amount. Does an increase in the amount imply an increase in the value? This question seems to be interesting at least on two grounds. First, it asks if an information system is like many commodities in economic analysis for which utility or value is often assumed or considered to be an increasing (or non-decreasing) function of their quantities. Secondly, the "consistency" of rankings will make it possible to use the amount of information (I) as a surrogate of the value of information (V) in information system selection. This possibility has a considerable appeal, at least in a practical sense, because of the practical difficulties of finding a suitable utility function and computing the optimal action and its

*This is as abstract. The entire article is published in Hitotsubashi Journal of Commerce and Management, Vol. 13, No. 1, June 1978. Hitotsubashi University, Kunitachi, Tokyo, Japan.

associated utility which the computation of $V$ requires. The computation of $I$ is simple and free from these difficulties.

The next section of the paper concentrates on the similar properties of the value and the amount of information. Both the value and the amount of information depend on the prior distribution and the information matrix $P$. Furthermore, both are defined in terms of the expected difference of certain quantities (i.e. utility for the value and the degree of uncertainty for the amount) between the case with an information system $P$ and the case without it. Therefore, it is perhaps natural to expect some similarities in their properties. Although much cannot be said without specifing the utility function and the decision situation of the decision-maker, we shall see that some very basic properties of the value of information are also present in the amount of information. This is somewhat encouraging if one would want to use the amount of information ($I$) as a surrogate of the value of information ($V$) in information systems selection. The major areas of similarity between $V$ and $I$ are: both $V$ and $I$ are non-negative, both $V$ and $I$ are additive, both $V$ and $I$ will never be increased by garbling of an information matrix, and both $V$ and $I$ are convex functions of $P$.

In section 3, we find that an information system which can be abstractly represented by an information matrix $P$ may be considered to consist of several basic information system elements or inputs which can be varied by an information system designer. Concretely, he does not change the message generating probability itself but manipulates some design parameters which eventually affect $P$. For example, in a sampling information system for statistical estimation the sample size and the sample precision are most likely design parameters. Then, in this light, the question of the consistency of ranking of information systems by $V$ and $I$ becomes a question of the consistency of the effects on $V$ and $I$ of changing design parameters. Section 3 is mostly mathematical and obtains conditions for the two rankings of information systems, one by $V$ and one by $I$, to be "consistent".

In section 4, we analyze the question of the identity of rankings of information systems by $V$ and by $I$ within the framework of the investment model with state contingent claims. The model was first proposed by Arrow and is now considered one of very general and basic frameworks of a pure exchange economy under uncertainty and investment in risky assets. Therefore, analysis of the identical ranking question in this particular framework is especially meaningful for accounting information evaluation. The relationship between $V$ and $I$ in this framework was first analyzed by Arrow. The major result of this section says, in short, that the rankings of information systems by $V$ and $I$ are identical over an arbitrary set of information systems if and only if the utility of income is of logarithmic form.

In the final section of the paper, we apply a theorem and its corollary developed in Section 3 and identify a class of information systems for which the ranking by $I$ cannot be reversed by the ranking by $V$ under a mild condition.

# A MATHEMATICAL ANALYSIS FOR DESIGNING AN EXCEPTION REPORTING SYSTEM*

by Masao Tsuji

## 1. Introduction

Contrary to the numerous and various studies on management information systems, there appears to be little organizational rationale behind the development of most of today's management information systems. Critical evidence continues to accrue that "the information systems of today are not, in general, what they are made out to be."[1]

Ackoff[2] argues that several assumptions commonly made by designers of management information systems are not justified in many cases and hence, lead to major deficiencies in the resulting systems. King and Cleland[3] claim that although modern management information systems are assumed to help the manager make better decisions, few are true management systems.

According to their observations, information systems have been shaped by improvements in existing data processing functions and have not significantly increased the decision making effectiveness of managers.

More recently, Wildavsky[4] criticizes today's information systems as "un-theoretical, non-organizational, a-historical" and "really made up of dumb data." Hedberg and Jönsson express a similar view and state that:

---

[1]Swanson (1979) p. 237.

[2]Ackoff (1969).

[3]King and Cleland (1971).

[4]Wildavsky (1978).



*This is an abstract of the complete article written by Masao Tsuji.

> It appears that many modern information systems dysfunctionally add to organizations' inertia. Access to more information and more advanced decision aids does not necessarily make decision makers better informed or more able to decide.[5]

Where do these deficiencies result from? Designers of management information systems are inclined to conceive that supplying information to decision makers is a good thing in-and-of itself. This seemingly well accepted notion will be challenged by the following considerations:

1) the problems of information overload,

2) the problem of processing information by decision makers, and

3) the fact that all information has a cost.

The viewpoint which has motivated this paper is the importance of shifting the emphasis of the information system design from supplying relevant information to eliminating irrelevant, unimportant information. The purpose of this paper is to develop evaluation methods for particular types of information and decision systems, and to investigate solutions for designing systems which can reduce information overload and be economically more efficient than current systems. Several mathematical models will be examined on the basis of recent developments in the area of inquiry known as "information economics" to solve these problems.

---

[5]Hedberg and Jönsson (1978) p. 48.

2. Deficiencies in the Development of Information Systems

It is generally recognized that the amount of information inputs and the methods of their provision influence the utilization of information provided form an information system. Information is utilized to enable a decision maker to make informed judgments and decisions. For the information to be useful, it must bear upon or be usefully associated with the decision which it is designed to facilitate or with the result which it is aiming to produce. The more closely information provided is attuned with a decision maker's needs, the more useful it will be in producing the desired result. Consequently, information and its method of reporting exert influence on designated decisions. For these influences to be exerted effectively, relevant information must be available and in a certain form and time for it to be useful.

According to Ackoff[6] and others, however, most managers suffer more from an overabundance of irrelevant information, while lacking a good deal of information which they should have. They receive more data than they can possibly absorb even if they spend all their time trying to do so. In short, they suffer from a so-called information overload. As a result, they must spend a great deal of time sorting the relevant from the irrelevant and searching for the kernels in the relevant documents.

Humans have limited capabilities for processing data. Beyond some point it becomes physically impossible to assimilate and react to incremented messages. Even modest increases in the amount of data provided could worsen decision effectiveness because of psychological effects. Increased information levels increase the perceived complexity of the

---

[6]Ackoff (1967).

environment. According to abundant psychological testing evidence, such changes in perceived environmental complexities induce change in the decision maker's cognitive processing capabilities.[7] These cognitive processing changes, in turn, can decrease the effectiveness of decision making causing the decision maker to revert to a more concrete conceptual level in an attempt to cope with a new, more complex environment.[8]

Certain relevant reports that are required to improve decision making effectiveness tend to be taken by many system designers as "given." In real decision making situations, however, managers in an organization may not want to collect all the relevant data that is available or make use of the information they process. According to Cyert and March[9], managers in a typical firm do not scan all alternatives or have complete information about the alternatives selected. The time factor may be critical: the time limit of most decisions demand to be taken on even without its complete information. Also, it has been suggested that searching for data is initiated in response to a number of factors, for example, when existing decisions seem to be unsatisfactory or when a problem is obscure.

An additional negative effect on the emphasis of supplying information is the problem of economic inefficiency. All information has a cost. Information should be treated as an economic commodity whose acquisition constitutes a problem of economic choice. This conception draws the inference that information should be obtained or supplied only if the benefits from its use can be justified as greater than or equal to its cost.

---

[7]Schroder, Driver, and Straufert (1967).

[8]Driver and Staufert (1969).

[9]Cyert and March (1965).

These considerations suggest that the conception of managers supplying information is a good thing in-and-of itself needs to be modified. The amount of information inputs and the way of providing them are important factors which affect not only information utilization and decision quality, but also, resource allocation in an organization.

The problem of information overload is especially crucial to the development of management information systems. As implied by the term, information overload is caused by the amount of information inputs which are greater than those which can be processed adequately. One efficient solution is to alleviate the situation by reducing the information inputs without any critical loss of the benefits yielded if such reduction has not been undertaken. It is important to note that this solution is consistent with the results of behavioral studies on human information processing which show that managers do indeed develop heuristics to reduce the amount of information processed.

## 3. An Exception Reporting System

This paper is based on the premise that in many modern organizations the problem of information system design should be primarily oriented toward the process of filtering, extracting, and condensing information, rather than on the generation, storage, and retrieval of information. The need is to make decision makers aware of that portion of the total set of information which is relevant to their decisions and to focus their attention on situations requiring their judgments and interventions. We refer to this type of information system as a management-by-exception reporting system, or simply an exception reporting system.

An exception reporting system is designed on the basis of the management-by-exception principle. Management-by-exception is one of the basic principles of management which has been widely accepted by current classical theorists. Generally, it states that decisions which recur frequently and are less important should be reduced to a routine and only those important issues or those which are non-recurring should be referred to focus on the decision maker's attention.

The idea behind the exception principle is the economic allocation of organization resources; an organization must economize its resources by dealing only with exceptional matters which have significant consequences on organization effectiveness.

Massie states that:

> Generally, the exception princple has been important to the development of the process of delegation of authority. It is basic to the generalization that all decisions should be made at the lowest organization level commensurating with personal ability and availability of information. It becomes useful in the development of systems for handling work. Of all the classical concepts, it probably comes closest to being a basic princple valid in many situations.[10]

Filtering or extracting is an essential function of the exception principle, applied to a management information system. Only those items which deserve attention to require action are singled out. This essentially involves a search for selected information, or the scanning of a given set of data in order to identify a subset with predetermined attributes.

The term exception reporting system covers certain organizational information-decision systems whereby the decision about a given action variable is normally made as a routine, but may be made on the basis of

---

[10]Massie (1965) pp. 377-8.

more information if the original information variables take on <u>exceptional</u> values.

Before giving a precise definition of an exception reporting system, the following description may be helpful. Assume that the range of possible values of uncertain variable x is divided into two parts, "ordinary" values and "exceptional" values. Let R denote a set of exceptional values. If, in a particular instance, an information evaluator who designs and selects the information system observes x to be ordinary, that is, not in R, then he does not provide a decision maker with that information, and the decision maker deals with the case as a routine. On the other hand, if the information evaluator observes x to be exceptional, that is, in R, then he reports that value to the decision maker. The decision maker then makes his decision on the basis of the exceptional observations.

More precisely, the structure of an exception reporting system, denoted by $\eta_e$, is defined as follows:

$$\eta_e = \begin{cases} \text{constant (independent of } x) & \text{if } x \varepsilon R \\ x & \text{if } x \varepsilon R \end{cases} \qquad (3.1)$$

where x is the state of an uncertain environment and R is a given subset of the real line (the set of exceptional values).

From the previous discussion about information structures, we notice that the structure of an exception reporting system defines a class of incomplete information structures which contain the finest and coarsest information structures.

The finest information structure, called complete information structure generally, is defined mathematically by

$$\eta_c = \{ x \} \qquad \text{for all } x \text{ in } X. \qquad (3.2)$$

On the other hand, the coarsest information structure, called null information structure generally, is given by

$$\eta_n = \text{constant (independent of x)} \quad \text{for all x in X.} \quad (3.3)$$

A decision rule based on the null information structure becomes a routine. However, if this structure is incorporated into the exception reporting system, this part informs the decision maker that the observed value of x is not exceptional.

## 4. An Exception Reporting System for Production: A Uniform Distribution Case

Consider a problem to select among alternative information structures which support the production manager's decision to determine an optimal output a* when product demand x is uncertain. Assume that x is distributed uniformly over the interval [0, 100], as shown in Figure 4.1. The payoff function is defined as follows:

$$u = \omega(x,a) = ka - g(x,a),$$

where

$$g(x,a) = \begin{cases} \alpha(x - a) & \text{if } x - a \geq 0 \\ \beta(x - a) & \text{if } x - a < 0. \end{cases} \quad (4.1)$$

In the above functions, parameter k is the marginal revenue per unit of product and parameter $\alpha$ represents the penalty of underproduction whereas $\beta$ represents that of overproduction.

Alternative information structures may be characterized by a different number n of subintervals of equal length into which the whole interval [0, 100] is partitioned. For example, let n = 1 representing the null information structure. The manager will not be informed at all of the demand for the product. If n = $\infty$, it means that he has the complete information strucutre which enables him to predict the demand precisely.

Figure 4.1. Uniform Distribution

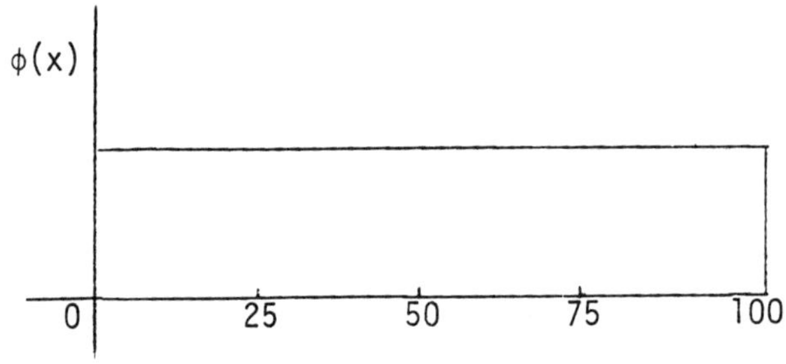


$$\phi(x) = \begin{cases} \frac{1}{100} & \text{if } 0 \leq x \leq 100 \\ 0 & \text{otherwise} \end{cases}$$

Under the null information structure $\eta_n$, the manager seeks the optimal action which yields the maximum expected payoff.

Next, we consider the complete information structure in which the manager is informed about the demand for the product. Obviously, the best production decision is $a^* = x$ under this structure. In general, overproduction causes the manager to incur the costs of inventory and expenses of disposing the quantities overproduced. If the marginal revenue were larger than the penalty cost of overproduction, the manager would be better off producing as much as possible.

Now, consider a discriminatory information structure. For example, let $n = 2$ and the whole interval [0, 100] be divided equally into the two subintervals. Under this structure, the manager will be told only whether the demand will be larger than 50 or not. Under this situation, it is possible for us to determine that complete information is twice as valuable as discriminatory information in terms of the gross value for this particular problem. This differential value gives the decision maker a guideline to evaluate these information structures when he takes into consideration information costs.

Finally, we investigate the information structure of an exception reporting system, which is defined as

$$\eta_e(x) = \begin{cases} x & \text{if } 0 \leq x \leq 25 \quad \text{or} \quad 75 \leq x \leq 100 \\ \text{constant otherwise} \end{cases} \tag{4.2}$$

The exceptional range R in this structure includes the lower interval [0, 25] and the upper interval [75, 100]. The manager will be informed of the uncertain, future demand of the product only when $x \in R$.

If x falls in the exceptional range, the informed optimal decision is written as $a^* = x$. If x is not in R, that is $25 < x < 75$, the manager cannot identify the exact quantities of demand, but can recognize that x will not have exceptional values. The best decision he should make is to produce the quantities that maximize the expected value of his payoff function given that $25 < x < 75$.

How efficient the exception information structure is in comparison with the complete information structure may be an interesting question to ask. It turns out that the answer depends on penalty costs of under- and over-production. As the penalty costs of underproduction rise, it is better to enlarge the exceptional ranges. Conversely, as the penalty of overproduction rises, it is better to shorten the exception ranges.

We also find that complete information brings much higher benefits when $75 \leq x \leq 100$ than when $0 \leq x \leq 25$. This fact, or course, results from particular forms of the payoff function as well as the probability distribution function. As far as this example is concerned, we may correctly conjecture that we receive higher expected benefits by setting the exceptional ranges as [50, 75] and [75, 100] rather than [0, 25] and [75, 100].

## 5. A Quadratic Function of a Single Decision Variable

The models used to derive the conclusions in this and the following are adapted from those developed by Marschak and Radner.[11] They describe the properties of decreasing returns with a quadratic approximation. The payoff depends upon the environment variable x (input price measured from its mean level) and the decision variable a (input quantity measured from that level which is the best one at the mean input price).

First, under the complete information structure, the decision maker is kept informed of the price variable x. Second, on the other hand, under the null information structure the decision maker receives no information about the price.

If, in a particular instance, an information evaluator observes x to be exceptional, he will inform the decision maker of its exceptional value. The decision maker will choose the best action for the state which the information signal represents. On the other hand, if x is observed to be not exceptional, that is, $x \in \tilde{R}$, the decision maker will make his decision based upon a priori information. It is not necessary to investigate the exact value of x in this instance. Under this structure it is sufficient that the information evaluator observes x to be not exceptional.

## 6. A Quadratic Function of Two Decision Variables

In this section we extend the previous analysis to the case in which two decision variables have to be determined by using alternative information structures. This case brings out the problem of organizational structure: decentralization vs. centralization.

---

[11] Marschak and Radner (1972).

In the centralized organization, a single decision maker may decide upon two physically distinct action variables: he may choose simultaneously the values of two variables on the basis of some information about uncertain states of environment. On the other hand, in the decentralized organization each decision maker decides upon only one of the action variables on the basis of his individual information. If a communication system is established between the two decision makers, it results in providing them with the same information on which their decisions are based. When there exists complementarity between two actions, error-free communication will never decrease the benefits.

The previous definition of the structure of an exception reporting system can be extended to the case where there exist more than one environmental variable. For each variable i, the exceptional set $R_i$ may be specified. We define this information structure as

$$\eta_e(x) = \begin{cases} x_i & \text{if } x_i \in R_i \\ \tilde{R}_j & \text{if } x_j \in \tilde{R}_j. \end{cases} \tag{6.1}$$

Since we have two environmental variables in our example, this information structure provides four kinds of information signals,

$$\eta_e(x) = \begin{cases} x_1 \text{ and } x_2 & \text{if } x_1 \in R_1 \text{ and } x_2 \in R_2 \\ x_1 \text{ and } \tilde{R}_2 & \text{if } x_1 \in R_1 \text{ and } x_2 \in \tilde{R}_2 \\ \tilde{R}_1 \text{ and } x_2 & \text{if } x_1 \in \tilde{R}_1 \text{ and } x_2 \in R_2 \\ \tilde{R}_1 \text{ and } \tilde{R}_2 & \text{if } x_1 \in \tilde{R}_1 \text{ and } x_2 \in \tilde{R}_2. \end{cases} \tag{6.2}$$

Suppose that each exceptional set $R_i$ is specified as symmetrical around the mean of $x_i$. In addition, we assume that $x_i$ which have symmetrical distributions with means zero and variances $s_i$ are statistically independent.

In the first case of $x_1 \in R_1$ and $x_2 \in R_2$, both variables belong to the exceptional ranges. The exact values of them are informed before the decisions are made. The payoff function to be maximized is the same as in the case of complete information structure. Second, when $x_1 \in R_1$ and $x_2 \in \tilde{R}_2$, the exact value of $x_1$, but not $x_2$ is provided before the decisions are made. In this case $x_2$ is known to be not exceptional and only the range of $x_2$ can be determined. For the third case in which $x_1 \varepsilon R_1$ and $x_2 \varepsilon R_2$, $x_2$ is correctly informed, but $x_1$ is known to be ordinal. The situation is just opposite to the second case. Finally, when both variables are known to be not exceptional, the actions become "routine."

## 7. Concluding Remarks

This paper has been based on the premise that the major problem in the design of information systems is the filtration of relevant information from irrelevant information and elimination of the latter.

In the management literature there have been several articles and fragmentary statements dealing with this subject. None of them, however, contain more than simple rules of thumb. In addition, the literature on the design of information systems seldom considers explicitly the function of filtration or extraction. This lack of the literature may be attributed to the fact that the exception principle has not attempted to define which activities and issues are routine and which are exceptional. As a result, it has been stated as a matter of degree depending on circumstances and subjective evaluation.

This paper has proposed conceptual models of an exception reporting system which incorporates some filtration mechanism. Since information economics is concerned with the trade-off between the cost of information and the value derived from that information, it can provide some criteria to decide which information sets to be eliminated. In short, the paper has sought a useful method for designing information systems which operationalizes the exception principle in management and integrates the principle with information economic precepts.

# REFERENCES

Ackoff, R. L. "Management Misinformation Systems," Management Science (December 1967), pp. 147-56.

Cyert, R. M. and J. G. March, A Behavioral Theory of the Firm (Prentice-Hall, 1965).

Driver, M. J. and S. Streufert, "Integrative Complexity: An Approach to Individuals and Group as Information-Processing Systems," Administrative Science Quarterly (June 1969), pp. 272-85.

Hedberg, B. and S. Jönsson, "Designing Semi-Confusing Information Systems for Orgnaizations in Changing Environments," Accounting, Organizations and Society, Vol. 3, No. 1, 1978, pp. 47-64.

King, W. R. and D. I. Cleland, "Manager-Analyst Teamwork in MIS," Business Horizons (April 1971), pp. 59-68.

Marschak, J. and R. Radner, Economic Theory of Teams (Yale University Press, 1972).

Massie, J. L., "Management Theory," in J. G. March ed., Handbook of Organization (Rand McNally, 1965), pp. 387-422.

Schroder, H. M., M. J. Driver, and S. Streufert, Human Information Processing (Hold, Rinehart and Winston, 1967).

Swanson, E. B., "The Two Faces or Organizational Information," Accounting, Organizations and Society, Vol. 3, No. 3/4, pp. 237-46.

Wildavsky, A., "Policy Analysis Is What Information Systems Are Not," Accounting, Organizations and Society, Vol. 3, No. 1, 1978, pp. 77-88.

# AN APPLICATION OF INPUT-OUTPUT ANALYSIS TO A PROCESS COST SYSTEM

Kyosuke Sakate

## 1. Introduction

The purpose of this paper is to combine two lines of progress in applying input-output analysis to managerial planning and control techniques, in the context of process costing.[1]

An improvement of departmental costing which incorporates reciprocal cost allocations applying a matrix algebra approach was proposed by Williams & Griffin[2] and Churchill.[3] Manes then presented a theoretical objection to both approaches for not equalizing total service department costs with allocated costs. He supported his argument by presenting his own model referred to as "the net service model."[4] Livingstone showed that Manes' method was not, in fact, different from Williams & Griffin and Churchill but was simply another way of expressing the same model.[5]

---

[1]Many persons provided numerous and invaluable help to the author in the form of discussions and suggestions which formulated the idea of this work. Gratitude is owed to Professor Gerhard G. Mueller and Professor Gary L. Sundem of the University of Washington for their guidance and direction while the author was a Visiting Scholar at the University during 1977-1978.

The first draft of this paper was significantly improved by continued comments and criticisms from Professors Sadao Ikeda and Masahisa Fukushima, and Associate Professor Yukio Itagagi, of Soka University, Japan.

[2]Williams & Griffin [1964].

[3]Churchill [1964].

[4]Manes [1965].

[5]Livingstone [1968].

Minch & Petri realized the difference between Williams & Griffin's model and Manes' model is simply due to the timing of credits for services performed--before or after charges for services received.[6] Admitting Manes' model as theoretically preferable, because it allows simultaneity of credits and charges, they presented their new model from a practical point of view, from which a matrix inversion is easily attainable.

After comparison of the three models, Kaplan pointed out that Manes' model and Minch & Petri's model would lead to a misleading conclusion, while Churchill's model was derived from an underlying economic model of the firm's production process and consequently produced allocations useful for managerial decisions.[7]

On the other hand, using numerical examples, Ijiri exhibited a method of deriving various useful data by applying an input-output analysis to cost data.[8] Livingstone also demonstrated the usefulness of an input-output analysis for planning and decision making, and presented the generality of its framework to include a matrix cost allocation model as a special case.[9]

In spite of the progress achieved by the papers designated above, the applicability of input-output analysis to the generally accepted cost system is not established because of some difficulties. The major difficulty arises from the existence of a work in process, lost units, and semi-finished products under the situation of actual costing. In

---

[6]Minch & Petri [1972].

[7]Kaplan [1973].

[8]Ijiri [1968].

[9]Livingstone [1969].

order to show one way of resolving this problem, a process costing model has been constructed based on input-output analysis.

## 2. Assumptions and Definitions

Let's assume that:

a) a model factory consists of r manufacturing departments and (n-r) service departments both of which have a single "cost center" in each;

b) the manufacturing departments have seven classes of input-work-in-process, defective work, transferred product, direct material, direct labor, primary allocated overhead and offered service--while the service departments have two classes; primary allocated overhead and offered service--shown in Table 1;

c) each of n departments yields outputs (products or services) of a single kind so that we may deal with homogeneous outputs;

d) the manufacturing departments have essentially five types of outputs classified as a finished product, transferred product, semi-finished product, work-in-process, and lost unit, while the service departments have one type of output--offered service--shown in Table 2;

e) the service department produce specific service which is offered to the service departments and the manufacturing departments.

An essential condition for input-output costing is homogeneity of output in every department. The assumption in (d) seems to be inconsistent with this requirement. However, computation of output in equivalent units of work performed will be a strong device to meet this requirement. In this sense, we can compose an input-output table which has a single column of final output including both the completed and incompleted products. This is ambiguous, however, since the meaning of final products in daily use covers the category of finished products but covers neither work-in-process nor lost units. Accordingly, it is reasonable to prepare a different column for each.

As in input, some features in the accounting process should also be taken into consideration. The defective work in Table 1 is related to the lost unit in Table 2. Once we obtain a cost figure for the lost units, further division of the figure should be made to attach the divided figures to various kinds of lost unit, for example, waste, damaged work, etc. Some portion of the lost unit referred to as "defective work" will be added direct material and/or reprocessed during the coming period.[10] Thus, the defective work in Table 1 is treated as input at the beginning of the period.

Furthermore, we should note that primary distribution of factory overhead to n department will be completed before we compose an input-output table. Theoretically, primary overhead allocation should be made based on the fact that variable components should be made based on the fact that variable components are consumed by activities performed while fixed components are incurred in relation to the existence of the activity capacity prepared. However, this distinction is considerably troublesome

[10]Strictly speaking, another type of defective work should be recognized. Namely, there are some defective units being reprocessed within the same period. These defective units may be regarded as self-consumed products in the manufacturing department. However, for simplication purposes, these units are excluded from input as well as output in this paper.

Table 1

Classification of Input[11]

| | Input at the Beginning of a Period | Input during the Period |
|---|---|---|
| Manufacturing Department | Work in Process (*)<br>Defective Work (*) | Transferred Product (**)<br>Direct Materials (*)<br>Direct Labor (*)<br>Overhead (primary) (*)<br>Offered Service |
| Service Dept. | | Overhead (primary) (*)<br>Offered Service (**) |

[11]Two categories are distinguished from each other using single and double asterisks which are referred to as the exogenous factor (primary) input and endogenous factor (intermediate) input where input-output analysis is applied.

Table 2

Classification of Output[12]

<table>
<tr><td colspan="2"></td><td>Fully Completed</td><td>Partially Completed</td></tr>
<tr><td rowspan="2">Manufacturing Department</td><td>Final Depart-ment</td><td>Finished Product (*)</td><td>Work in Process (*)<br>Lost Unit[13] (*)</td></tr>
<tr><td>Inter-mediate Dept.</td><td>Transferred Product (**)<br>Semi-Finished Product (*)</td><td>Work in Process (*)<br>Lost Unit (*)</td></tr>
<tr><td colspan="2">Service Department</td><td></td><td>Offered Service (**)</td></tr>
</table>

[12]Two categories are also distinguished from each other using single and double asterisks which are referred to as final demand (output) and intermediate demand (output) where Input-Output is applied.

[13]Lost units in a broader sense typically include wasted units, totally ruined units, by-products and damaged units which require subsequent rework (see Corcoran [1978], pp. 192-94).

for reflection in practice of computing distribution rates. Thus, we start from a secondary distribution of overhead in order to neglect this difficulty in this paper.

Along with these assumptions and devices, complicated transactions among the departments during the period and a related situation at the beginning as well as the end of the period is displayed in Figure 1 and Table 3 shown below.

In Figure 1, the circles and triangles drawn represent the manufacturing departments and service departments, respectively. Services offered to the manufacturing departments and the service department are indicated by the solid lines while the transferred products from one manufacturing department but not transferred to the succeeding departments. The semi-finished products are sold in a market or stocked for the purpose of future material inventory adjustment.

Figure 1

A Schematic Presentation of Physical Flows

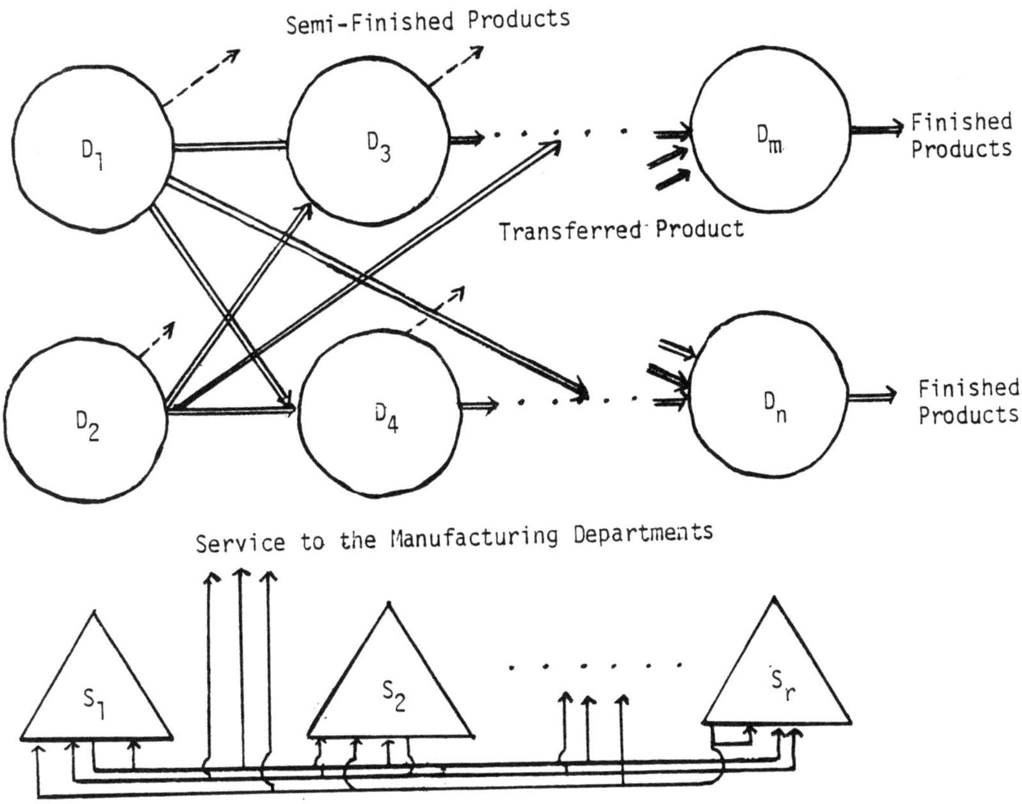

Table 3

Physical Input-Output Table

| Output / Output | | | Intermediate Input Unit: Manufacturing Department 1 | 2 | 3.....r | Service Dept. r+1 | n | Final Output $\underline{f}_1$ | $\underline{f}_2$ | $\underline{f}_3$ | $\underline{f}_4$ | $\underline{g}$ |
|---|---|---|---|---|---|---|---|---|---|---|---|---|
| Intermediate Output | Manufacturing Department | 1 | 0 | $a_{12}$ | $a_{13} \cdots a_{1r}$ | 0 | | $f_{11}$ | $f_{12}$ | $f_{13}$ | $f_{14}$ | $g_1$ |
| | | 2 | 0 | 0 | $a_{23} \cdots a_{2r}$ | | | $f_{21}$ | $f_{22}$ | $f_{23}$ | $f_{24}$ | $g_2$ |
| | | 3 | 0 | 0 . | 0 · | | | . | . | . | . | . |
| | | . | | 0 | | | | . | . | . | . | . |
| | | . | | | | | | . | . | . | . | . |
| | | . | | | $a_{r-1,\ r}$ | | | $f_{r-1,1}$ | $f_{r-1,2}$ | $f_{r-1,3}$ | $f_{r-1,4}$ | $g_{r-1}$ |
| | | r | 0 | 0 | 0.....0 | | | $f_{r1}$ | $f_{r2}$ | $f_{r3}$ | $f_{r4}$ | $g_r$ |
| | Service Dept. | r+1 | $a_{r+1,1}$ | $a_{r+1,2}$ | $\cdots a_{r+1,r}$ | $a_{r+1,r+1}$ | $\cdots a_{r+1,n}$ | 0 | 0 | 0 | 0 | $g_{r+1}$ |
| | | . | . | . | . | . | . | . | . | . | . | . |
| | | . | . | . | . | . | . | . | . | . | . | . |
| | | n | $a_{n1}$ | $a_{n2} \cdots$ | $a_{nr}$ | $a_{n,r+1}$ | $\cdots a_{nn}$ | 0 | 0 | 0 | 0 | $g_n$ |
| Primary Input Unit | Direct Materia | 1 | $q_{11}$ | $q_{12} \cdots$ | $q_{1r}$ | 0 . . . | 0 | | | | | |
| | | ⋮ | ⋮ | ⋮ | ⋮ | ⋮ | ⋮ | | | | | |
| | | h | $q_{h1}$ | $q_{h2} \cdots$ | $q_{hr}$ | 0 . . . | 0 | | | | | |
| | Direct Labor | 1 | $u_{11}$ | $u_{12} \cdots$ | $u_{1r}$ | 0 | 0 | | | | | |
| | | ⋮ | ⋮ | ⋮ | ⋮ | ⋮ | ⋮ | | | | | |
| | | $\ell$ | $u_{\ell 1}$ | $u_{\ell 2} \cdots$ | $u_{\ell r}$ | 0 . . . | 0 | | | | | |
| | Over-head | 1 | $v_{11}$ | $v_{12} \cdots$ | $v_{1r}$ | $v_{1,r+1}$ · · | $v_{1n}$ | | | | | |
| | | ⋮ | ⋮ | ⋮ | ⋮ | ⋮ | ⋮ | | | | | |
| | | m | $v_{m1}$ | $v_{m2} \cdots$ | $v_{mr}$ | $v_{m,r+1}$ · · | $v_{mn}$ | | | | | |
| | Beginning Inventory | ${}^t\underline{F}_1$ | $F_{11}$ | $F_{12} \cdots$ | $F_{1r}$ | 0 . . . | 0 | | | | | |
| | | ${}^t\underline{F}_2$ | $F_{21}$ | $F_{22} \cdots$ | $F_{2r}$ | 0 . . . | 0 | | | | | |

The variables appearing in Table 3 are defined as follows:

$a_{ij}$ = physical units of the completed products or produced service in the i-th department transferred or offered to the j-th department--intermediate output of the i-th and intermediate input to the j-th department;

$f_{i1}$ = physical equivalent units of the work in process at the end of the period in the i-th department;

$f_{i2}$ = physical equivalent lost units in the i-th department;

$f_{i3}$ = physical units of the semi-finished products in the i-th department;

$f_{i4}$ = physical units of the finished products in the final departments (in the technical sense);

$g_i$ = total equivalent physical units of all products or services produced in the i-th department;

$q_{ij}$ = physical values of the i-th direct materials consumed in the j-th manufacturing department;

$u_{ij}$ = physical values of the i-th direct labor consumed in the j-th manufacturing department;

$v_{ij}$ = monetary values of the i-th overhead primarily allocated to the j-th department;

$F_{ij}$ = physical equivalent units of the work in process at the beginning of a given period in the j-th manufacturing department which is calculated as $f_{i1}$ at the end of the previous period; and,

$F_{2j}$ = physical equivalent units of defective products at the beginning of a given period in the j-th manufacturing department--a portion of the lost units $f_{i2}$ at the end of the previous period.

Further, we introduce some matrices and vectors to operate these variables:

$A = [a_{ij}]$ . . . n by n physical input-output matrix;

$\underline{f}_1 = [f_{i1}]$ . . . n dimensional column vector of the ending work in process;

$\underline{f}_2 = [f_{i2}]$ . . . n dimensional column vector of the lost units;

$\underline{f}_3 = [f_{i3}]$ . . . n dimensional column vector of the semi-finished products;

$\underline{f}_4 = [f_{i4}]$ . . . n dimensional column vector of the finished products;

$\underline{g} = [g_i]$ . . . n dimensional column vector of the total equivalent outputs;

$Q = [q_{ij}]$ . . . h by n direct material matrix;

$U = [u_{ij}]$ . . . $\ell$ by n direct labor matrix;

$V = [v_{ij}]$ . . . m by n primary overhead matrix;

$^t\underline{F}_1 = [F_{1j}]$ . . . n dimensional row vector of the beginning work in process; and,

$^t\underline{F}_2 = [F_{2j}]$ . . . n dimensional row vector of the beginning defective products.

3. Process Costing Model

Cost measurement related to the products produced is an inevitable function of cost accounting. One of the dominant rules of cost measurement for external reports is to allocate and attach all costs incurred for production of goods and services to the products manufactured based on benefits received by the specific products. Our major concern is to investigate whether or not the proposed model satisfies this requirement in the context of process costing.

Since the physical equivalent units are determined differently in calculation of direct material costs from calculation of conversion costs, we should prepare two classes of matrices and vectors. Hereafter, single prime or double prime matrices and vectors as well as variables are used in calculating direct material costs and conversion costs, respectively, although there are some exceptions. When the independent variables are given the same values in both calculations, we use non-prime matrices and vectors. Similarly, in the case of the sum value of direct material and conversion costs, we also use non-prime matrices and vectors.

Let ${}^t\underline{c} = [c_i]$ be a n dimensional row vector of manufacturing costs (measured as input costs) which is divided into ${}^t\underline{c}_1 = [c_{1i}]$ and ${}^t\underline{c}_2 = [c_{2i}]$. The former and the latter stand for direct material costs and conversion costs, respectively. Moreover, let ${}^t\underline{p}_1 = [p_{i1}]$ and ${}^t\underline{p}_2[p_{i2}]$ be a h dimensional row vector of unit prices for direct materials and a $\ell$ dimensional row vector of wage rates of direct labor, respectively. The unit cost of the equivalent output units calculated at the end of the previous period will be regarded as a unit price of the beginning work in process as well as the defective products.

Using these units costs, we introduce a diagonal matrix $D_p$ by

$$D_p \text{ is diag } [p_1, \ldots, p_n],$$

where $p_i$ is the unit cost of the equivalent output units of the i-th department in the previous period.

Now, we obtain the following expressions:

$$^t\underline{c} = {}^t\underline{c}_1 + {}^t\underline{c}_2 \tag{1}$$

$$^t\underline{c}_1 = {}^t\underline{p}_1 Q + {}^t\underline{F}_1' D_p + {}^t\underline{F}_2' D_{p'}, \quad \text{and} \tag{2}$$

$$^t\underline{c}_2 = {}^t\underline{p}_2 U + {}^t\underline{e}_m V + {}^t\underline{F}_1'' D_p + {}^t\underline{F}_2'' D_{p''} \tag{3}$$

where $^t\underline{e}_m$ is an m dimensional row vector whose elements are all unity.

Then we continue and attach two clases of incurred costs--direct material costs and conversion costs--to the various kinds of products. It is the first step to find a ratio on which one department offers its products or services to the other. In proportion to this ratio, the costs incurred in one department should be charged to the others. In other words, output costs of one department should be understood as input costs of the others.

First, let's consider the situation of handling direct material costs. We shall divide each row element of A, $\underline{f}_1$, $\underline{f}_2$, $\underline{f}_3$, and $\underline{f}_4$ by a corresponding row element of $\underline{g}$ to obtain the following output coefficient:

$$\frac{a_{ij}'}{g_i'} = m_{ij}', \quad \frac{f_{i1}'}{g_i'} = m_{i1}', \quad \frac{f_i'}{g_i'} = m_{i2}', \quad \frac{f_{i3}}{g_i'} = m_{i3}', \text{ and } \frac{f_{i4}}{g_i'} = m_{i4}'.$$

For convenience, we introduce the following matrix and vectors:

$M'$[14] $= [m'_{ij}]$ . . . n by n physical output coefficients matrix of transferred or offered products or services;

$\underline{m}'_1 = [m'_{i1}]$ . . . n dimensional physical outputs coefficients column vector of work in process;

$\underline{m}'_2 = [m'_{i2}]$ . . . n dimensional physical output coefficients column vector of lost units;

$\underline{m}'_3 = [m'_{i3}]$ . . . n dimensional physical output coefficients column vector of semi-finished products;

$\underline{m}'_4 = [m'_{i4}]$ . . . n dimensional physical output coefficients column vector of finished products.

---

[14]Although it is clear by looking at Table 3 that many elements should be zero in matrix M', and other column vectors, we continue to use the n by n matrix and n dimensional vectors for general adaptability of the model.

If we introduce the matrix $D'_g$ by diag $[g'_1, \ldots, g'_n]$, then the following simple relations are obtained:

$$
\begin{aligned}
M' &= D_{g'}^{-1} A \quad , \\
\underline{m}'_1 &= D_{g'}^{-1} \underline{f}'_1 \quad , \\
\underline{m}'_2 &= D_{g'}^{-1} \underline{f}'_2 \quad , \\
\underline{m}'_3 &= D_{g'}^{-1} \underline{f}'_3 \quad , \text{ and} \\
\underline{m}'_4 &= D_{g'}^{-1} \underline{f}'_4 \quad .
\end{aligned}
\tag{4}
$$

Let $X' = [X'_i]$ $(i = 1, \ldots, n)$ be a column vector which stands for the total amount of direct material costs in the i-th department. Moreover, let $K' = [k'_{ij}]$, $\underline{x}'_1 = [x'_{i1}]$, $\underline{x}'_2 = [x'_{i2}]$, $\underline{x}'_3 = [x'_{i3}]$, $\underline{x}'_4 = [x'_{i4}]$ be the n by n matrix and column vectors of dimension n, which represent direct material costs of the transferred products from the i-th department to the j-th one, work in process, lost units, semi-finished products, and finished products of the j-th department, respectively.

The total direct material costs of the j-th department is measured as a sum of direct material costs incurred in the j-th department and direct material costs of transferred products from others. The latter is simply derived from the multiplication of coefficient $m'_{ij}$ and total direct material costs of the i-th department. Thus we have the expression:

$$X' = \underline{c}_1 + {}^tM' \, X' \tag{5}$$

This equation is solved in the form

$$X' = [I - {}^tM']^{-1} \, \underline{c}_1 \tag{6}$$

provided[15] that there exists $[I - {}^tM']$.

---

[15]In the relations, ${}^tM'$ implies the transpose of $M'$ and I implies the identity matrix of dimension n. The condition is satisfied under the situation of "Productiveness." (See Sakate, forthcoming in May 1980).

Using the matrix and column vectors defined above in (4), we can easily obtain the matrix and column vectors of direct material costs of various products:

$$\begin{aligned} K' &= D_{x'}\, M' \quad , \\ \underline{x}'_1 &= D_{x'}\, \underline{m}'_1 \quad , \\ \underline{x}'_2 &= D_{x'}\, \underline{m}'_2 \quad , \\ \underline{x}'_3 &= D_{x'}\, \underline{m}'_3 \quad , \text{ and} \\ \underline{x}'_4 &= D_{x'}\, \underline{m}'_4 \end{aligned} \tag{7}$$

where $D_{x'}$ is diag $[x'_1, \text{mmm}, x'_n]$.

Then, we simply show the following relations related to conversion cost calculations in order to avoid redundancy:

$$\begin{aligned} M'' &= D^{-1}_{g''}\, A \quad , \\ \underline{m}''_1 &= D^{-1}_{g''}\, \underline{f}''_1 \quad , \\ \underline{m}''_2 &= D^{-1}_{g''}\, \underline{f}''_2 \quad , \\ \underline{m}''_3 &= D^{-1}_{g''}\, \underline{f}''_3 \quad , \text{ and} \\ \underline{m}''_4 &= D^{-1}_{g''}\, \underline{f}''_4 \quad . \end{aligned} \tag{8}$$

As for total conversion costs of the various final outputs, the following relation holds:

$$\underline{X}'' = \underline{c}_2 + {}^{t}M''\, \underline{X}'' \tag{9}$$

which is solved for X" in the form:

$$\underline{X}'' = [I - {}^{t}M'']^{-1}\, \underline{c}_2 \quad . \tag{10}$$

Similarly, in the case of direct material costs, various output conversion costs are obtained as:

$$\begin{aligned} K'' &= D_{x''}\, M'' \quad , \\ \underline{x}''_1 &= D_{x''}\, \underline{m}''_1 \quad , \\ \underline{x}''_2 &= D_{x''}\, \underline{m}''_2 \quad , \\ \underline{x}''_3 &= D_{x''}\, \underline{m}''_3 \quad , \text{ and} \\ \underline{x}''_4 &= D_{x''}\, \underline{m}''_4 \quad . \end{aligned} \tag{11}$$

Thus we obtain the cost figure results of the transferred products (K' + K"), work in process ($\underline{x}_1' + \underline{x}_1''$), the lost units ($\underline{x}_2' + \underline{x}_2''$), semi-finished products ($\underline{x}_3' + \underline{x}_3''$), finished products ($\underline{x}_4' + \underline{x}_4''$), and total outputs ($\underline{X}' + \underline{X}''$).

## 4. Reviewing the Model

Is it safe to say that our input-output model is rational to be applied in the accounting practice? We should first examine the accounting implication of the mathematical relationship among various matrices and vectors used in the model to answer this question. For this reason, we have composed an input-output table in terms of cost figures as shown below.

Table 4

Monetary Input-Output Table

| Output \ Input | | Transferred Input Cost | | | | | | Final Output Cost | | | | |
|---|---|---|---|---|---|---|---|---|---|---|---|---|
| | | 1 | 2 | 3..... | r | r+1 . . . | n | $\underline{x}_1$ | $\underline{x}_2$ | $\underline{x}_3$ | $\underline{x}_4$ | $\underline{X}$ |
| Transferred Output Cost | 1 | 0 | $k_{12}$ | $k_{13}$ | $k_{1r}$ | | | $x_{11}$ | $x_{12}$ | $x_{13}$ | $x_{14}$ | $X_1$ |
| | 2 | 0 | 0 | $k_{23}$ | $k_{2r}$ | | | $x_{21}$ | $x_{22}$ | $x_{23}$ | $x_{24}$ | $X_2$ |
| | 3 | 0 | 0 | 0 | . | | | . | . | . | . | . |
| | . | | | | . | 0 | | . | . | . | . | . |
| | . | | 0 | | . | | | . | . | . | . | . |
| | . | | | | $k_{r-1,r}$ | | | $x_{r-1,1}$ | $x_{r-1,2}$ | $x_{r-1,3}$ | $x_{r-1,4}$ | $X_{r-1}$ |
| | r | 0 | 0 | 0..... | 0 | | | $x_{r1}$ | $x_{r2}$ | $x_{r3}$ | $x_{r4}$ | $X_r$ |
| | r+1 | $k_{r+1,1}$ | $k_{r+1,2}$ | . . | $k_{r+1,r}$ | $k_{r+1,r+1}$ . . . | $k_{r+1,n}$ | 0 | 0 | 0 | 0 | $X_{r+1}$ |
| | . | . | . | | . | . | . | . | . | . | . | . |
| | . | . | . | | . | . | . | . | . | . | . | . |
| | . | . | . | | . | . | . | . | . | . | . | . |
| | . | . | . | | . | . | . | . | . | . | . | . |
| | n | $k_{r1}$ | $k_{n2}$ | . . . | $k_{nr}$ | $k_{n,r+1}$ . . . | $k_{nn}$ | 0 | 0 | 0 | 0 | $X_n$ |
| Primary Input Cost: $t_{\underline{C}}$ | $t_{\underline{c}_1}$ | $C_{11}$ | $C_{12}$ | . . . | $C_{1r}$, | 0 . . . | 0 | | | | | |
| | $t_{\underline{c}_2}$ | $C_{21}$ | $C_{22}$ | . . . | $C_{2r}$, | $C_{2,r+1}$ . | $C_{2n}$ | | | | | |
| Primary Input Cost: $t_{\underline{X}}$ | | $X_1$ | $X_2$ | . . . | $X_r$ , | $X_{r+1}$ . . | $X_n$ | | | | | |

First of all, we should check the justifiability of equations (5) and (9). This problem has been discussed in the context of reciprocal allocation of service departmental costs.[16] The main controversy is about the terminology of input and output costs which happens to reappear in our model. In equation (5) for example, the matrix X on the left hand side stands for total input costs of direct materials while X' on the right hand side stands for the total output cost of direct materials. To justify this method, we must show that there exists the additivity of row elements in Table 4 above the double line. Here, by additivity of row elements, we indicate the relation

$$\sum_{j=1}^{n} k_{ij} + \sum_{j=1}^{n} x_{ij} = X_i \qquad \text{for all i.}$$

We should start from the fundamental assumptions originally presented. The physical flows as assumed are summarized in Table 3. It should be emphasized again that there exists similar additivity for any row above the double line in Table 3 based on assumption (d) and (e) mentioned at the beginning of this paper. Consequently, the following basic relations hold:

$$\sum_{j=1}^{n} a_{ij} + f'_{i1} + f'_{i2} + f_{i3} + f_{i4} = g'_i \qquad \text{and}$$

$$\sum_{j=1}^{n} a_{ij} + f''_{i1} + f''_{i2} + f_{i3} + f_{i4} = g''_i \qquad \text{for all i.}$$

We rewrite these relations in the following manner:

$$A\,\underline{e}_n + [\underline{f}'_1, \underline{f}'_2, \underline{f}_3, \underline{f}_4]\,\underline{e}_n = \underline{g}' \quad \text{and} \tag{12}$$

$$A\,\underline{e}_n + [\underline{f}''_1, \underline{f}''_2, \underline{f}_3, \underline{f}_4]\,\underline{e}_n = \underline{g}'',$$

---

[16] Manes (1965).
Livingstone (1968).
Minchi and Petri (1972).

where $\underline{e}_n$ is a column vector of dimension n whose elements are all unity. From relations (12) and (13), we can derive the expressions:

$$\sum_{j=1}^{n} k'_{ij} + \sum_{j=1}^{4} x'_{ij} = X'_i \quad \text{and} \qquad (14)$$

$$\sum_{j=1}^{n} k''_{ij} + \sum_{j=1}^{4} x''_{ij} = X''_i \quad \text{for all i.} \qquad (15)$$

Because, relation (12) can be rewritten as:

$$D_{X'} D_{g'}^{-1} A \underline{e}_n + D_{X'} D_{g'}^{-1} [\underline{f}'_1, \underline{f}'_2, \underline{f}_3, \underline{f}_4] \underline{e}_n = D_{X'} D_{g'}^{-1} \underline{g}'$$

(by premultiplication of $D_{X'} D_{g'}^{-1}$)

$$D_{X'} M' \underline{e}_n + D_{X'} [\underline{m}'_1, \underline{m}'_2, \underline{m}'_3, \underline{m}'_4] \underline{e}_n = D_{X'} \underline{e}_n \quad \text{(by (4) )}$$

$$K' \underline{e}_n + [\underline{x}'_1, \underline{x}'_2, \underline{x}'_3, \underline{x}'_4] \underline{e}_n = \underline{X}' \quad \text{(by (7) )}$$

which is identical to (14).

Similarly, relation (13) leads to the following rewritten forms:

$$D_{X''} D_{g''}^{-1} A \underline{e}_n + D_{X''} D_{g''}^{-1} [\underline{f}''_1, \underline{f}''_2, \underline{f}_3, \underline{f}_4] \underline{e}_n = D_{X''} D_{g''}^{-1} \underline{g}''$$

(by premultiplication of $D_{X''} D_{g''}^{-1}$)

$$D_{X''} M'' \underline{e}_n + D_{X''} [\underline{m}''_1, \underline{m}''_2, \underline{m}''_3, \underline{m}''_4] \underline{e}_n = D_{X''} \underline{e}_n \quad \text{(by (8) )}$$

$$K'' \underline{e}_n + [\underline{x}''_1, \underline{x}''_2, \underline{x}''_3, \underline{x}''_4] \underline{e}_n = \underline{X}'' \quad \text{(by (11) )}$$

which is identical to (15).

Adding relation (14) to relation (15), we conclude that:

$$\sum_{j=1}^{n} (k'_{ij} + k''_{ij}) + \sum_{j=1}^{n} (x'_{ij} + x''_{ij}) = X'_i + X''_i \quad \text{for all i.}$$

Thus, it is proved that there is additivity of the rows in Table 4 above the double line as long as we accept the assumption briefly reformulated below:

Total physical units of output $\underline{g}_i$ is definable as the sum of transferred output units $(\sum_j a_{ij})$ and final output units $(\sum_j f_{ij})$.

In the field of accounting, this assumption is generally acceptable in the sense that accountants use the physical equivalent units as a basis of cost allocation.

Now, let's turn to another question concerning the model. Does an aggregated amount of all final output costs equal all primary input costs? As we have seen above, similar matrix operations are possible for conversion costs as for direct material costs. Accordingly, we will examine the problem only in the context of direct material costs. Let y and z be the total amount of primary input costs and final output costs, respectively.

It is clearly seen that y and z will be given as:

$$y = {}^t\underline{c}_1\ \underline{e}_n \qquad \text{and} \qquad (16)$$

$$z = {}^t\underline{e}_n\ [\underline{x}_1',\ \underline{x}_2',\ \underline{x}_3',\ \underline{x}_4']\ \underline{e}_n\ . \qquad (17)$$

We rewrite equation (17) as:

$$z = {}^t\underline{e}_n\ [D_{x'}\ \underline{m}_1',\ D_{x'}\ \underline{m}_2',\ D_{x'}\ \underline{m}_3',\ D_{x'}\ \underline{m}_4']\ \underline{e}_n \qquad \text{(by (7)\ )} \quad (18)$$

$$= {}^t\underline{e}_n\ D_{x'}\ [D_{g'}^{-1}\ \underline{f}_1',\ D_{g'}^{-1}\ \underline{f}_2',\ D_{g'}^{-1}\ \underline{f}_3,\ D_{g'}^{-1}\ \underline{f}_4]\ \underline{e}_n \quad \text{(by (4)\ )} \quad (19)$$

$$= {}^t\underline{x}'\ D_{g'}^{-1}\ [\underline{f}_1',\ \underline{f}_2',\ \underline{f}_3,\ \underline{f}_4]\ \underline{e}_n\ . \qquad (20)$$

On the other hand, we obtain the following expressions:

$$D_{g'}^{-1}\ [\underline{f}_1',\ \underline{f}_2',\ \underline{f}_3,\ \underline{f}_4]\ \underline{e}_n = D_{g'}^{-1}\ [\underline{g} - A\ \underline{e}_n] \qquad \text{(by (12)\ )} \quad (21)$$

$$= [I - D_{g'}^{-1}\ A]\ \underline{e}_n \qquad (22)$$

$$+\ [I - M']\ \underline{e}_n. \qquad \text{(by (4)\ )} \quad (23)$$

Further, we obtain the following relations:

$${}^t\underline{x} = {}^t\Big[[I - {}^tM']^{-1}\ \underline{c}_1\Big] \qquad (24)$$

$$= {}^t\underline{c}_1\ {}^t\Big[[I - {}^tM']^{-1}\Big] \qquad (25)$$

$$= {}^t\underline{c}_1\ \Big[{}^t[I - {}^tM']\Big]^{-1} \qquad (26)$$

$$= {}^t\underline{c}_1\ [I - M']^{-1}\ . \qquad (27)$$

Finally, substituting equations (23) and (27) into equation (20), we obtain the following:

$$z = {}^{t}\underline{c}_1 \, [I - M']^{-1} [I - M'] \, \underline{e}_n \tag{28}$$

which is simply arranged as:

$$z = {}^{t}\underline{c}_1 \, \underline{e}_n \tag{29}$$

$$= y \tag{30}$$

Thus, we proved that the total amount of final output costs is exactly equal to the total amount of primary input costs.

## 6. Conclusion

In this paper, the original input-output analysis developed in the field of economics is applied to a process cost system. The most remarkable advantage of this application is the separation of a technological system from a cost phenomena actually caused by the system, because various chains of cause and effect can be derived from the process of cost measurement using input-output analysis.

One of the ideas employed for the application is the expansion of a final output category to include work in process and lost units, although these outputs are not "final" as in the implied meaning of the word. At present, ramified calculations can be carried out instantly and economically. On the contrary, benefits of this application are to increase the accuracy and speed of cost calculations, leading to the usefulness of the cost system.

The proposed model can be linked with a budgeting model structured on input-output analysis. Modification should be made carefully in this case especially regarding physical input coefficients used in the budgeting model. Fixed cost components must be excluded from the model since these factors cannot be expressed in linear functions. To eliminate the restriction, we must develop a non-linear analysis applicable to a budgeting and costing model in the context of a process cost system.

# REFERENCES


Churchill, N. "Linear Algebra and Cost Allocation: Some Examples," The Accounting Review (October 1964), pp. 894-904.

Corcoran, A. W., Costs--Accounting, Analysis, and Control, John Wiley & Sons, 1978.

Ijiri, Y., "An Application of Input-Output Analysis to Some Problems in Cost Accounting," Management Accounting (April 1968), pp. 49-61.

Kaplan, R. S. "Variable and Self-Service Costs in Reciprocal Allocation Models," The Accounting Review (October 1973), pp. 738-48.

Livingstone, J. L. "Matrix Algebra and Cost Allocation," The Accounting Review (July 1968), pp. 503-508.

Livingstone, J. L. "Input-Output Analysis for Cost Accounting, Planning and Control," The Accounting Review (January 1969), pp. 48-64.

Manes, R. P., "Comment on Matrix Theory and Cost Allocation," The Accounting Review (July 1965), pp. 640-43.

Minch, R. & E. Petri, "Matrix Models of Reciprocal Service Cost Allocation," The Accounting Review (July 1972), pp. 576-80.

Sakate, K., "Some Problems of a Budgeting and Costing Model Structured on Input-Output Analysis," Technical Report Institute of Information Sciences, Soka University, Japan, forthcoming in May, 1980.

Williams, T. H. & C. H. Griffin, "Matrix Theory and Cost Allocation," The Accounting Review (July 1964), pp. 671-78.